Literacy and English

CfE First Level
Book 1C

Maddy Barnes
Series Editor: Gemma Meharg

HODDER
GIBSON
AN HACHETTE UK COMPANY

The Publishers would like to thank the following for permission to reproduce copyright material.

Acknowledgements

pp.14–15 'Sleeping Beauty' from *Rising Stars Vocabulary: Reception and Key Stage 1* by Siobhan Skeffington & Charlotte Raby, reproduced by permission of Rising Stars, an imprint of Hodder Education; **pp.34–6** 'How Do Your Senses Work?' from *Cracking Writing Year 3 Teacher's Guide* by Kate Ruttle reproduced by permission of Rising Stars, an imprint of Hodder Education; **p.51** 'The Teacher's Day in Bed' by David Orme © David Orme. Reproduced by permission of the author; **pp.63–4** extract from *The Disappearing Moon* by Simon Bartram, published by Templar Books, an imprint of Bonnier Books Ltd: *Bob and Barry's Lunar Adventures* by Simon Bartram. Text copyright © Simon Bartram, 2009. First published in the UK by Bonnier Books UK Ltd.; **pp.77–8** 'Garden Creatures' from *Cracking Writing Year 3 Teacher's Guide* by Kate Ruttle reproduced by permission of Rising Stars, an imprint of Hodder Education; **p.93** 'A Dream of Elephants' by Tony Mitton published by Plum (Scholastic 1998) and reproduced by permission of David Higham Associates on behalf of Tony Mitton; **pp.105–7** 'On Safari' by Nick Hunter from *Cracking Writing Year 4 Teacher's Guide* by Kate Ruttle reproduced by permission of Rising Stars, an imprint of Hodder Education; **p.121–3** Dragons' Kingdom advert from *Cracking Writing Year 4 Teacher's Guide* by Kate Ruttle reproduced by permission of Rising Stars, an imprint of Hodder Education; **p. 137 & 144** illustration from *Cracking Writing Year 4 Teacher's Guide* by Kate Ruttle reproduced by permission of Rising Stars, an imprint of Hodder Education; **p.138** 'When Daddy Fell Into the Pond' by Alfred Noyes reproduced by permission of The Estate of Alfred Noyes c/o The Society of Author.

Every effort has been made to trace all copyright holders, but if any have been inadvertently overlooked, the Publishers will be pleased to make the necessary arrangements at the first opportunity.

Although every effort has been made to ensure that website addresses are correct at time of going to press, Hodder Gibson cannot be held responsible for the content of any website mentioned in this book. It is sometimes possible to find a relocated web page by typing in the address of the home page for a website in the URL window of your browser.

Hachette UK's policy is to use papers that are natural, renewable and recyclable products and made from wood grown in well-managed forests and other controlled sources. The logging and manufacturing processes are expected to conform to the environmental regulations of the country of origin.

Orders

Orders: please contact Hachette UK Distribution, Hely Hutchinson Centre, Milton Road, Didcot, Oxfordshire, OX11 7HH. Telephone: +44 (0)1235 827827. Email education@hachette.co.uk Lines are open from 9 a.m. to 5 p.m., Monday to Friday. You can also order through our website: www.hoddereducation.co.uk. If you have queries or questions that aren't about an order, you can contact us at hoddergibson@hodder.co.uk

© Madeleine Barnes 2021

First published in 2021 by

TeeJay Publishers, an imprint of Hodder Gibson, which is part of the Hodder Education Group.

An Hachette UK Company

211 St Vincent Street

Glasgow, G2 5QY

Impression number	5	4	3	2	1
Year	2025	2024	2023	2022	2021

Cover illustration by Ai Higaki/D'Avila Illustration Agency

Illustrations by Aptara, Inc.

Typeset in VAG Rounded Std 18/20pt by Aptara, Inc.

Printed in Italy

A catalogue record for this title is available from the British Library.

ISBN: 978 1 3983 2827 3

MIX
Paper from responsible sources
FSC™ C104740
www.fsc.org

SCOTLAND EXCEL

We are an approved supplier on the Scotland Excel framework.

Schools can find us on their procurement system as:

TeeJay Publishers.

Contents

Term 2

Term 3

Introduction

How will I enjoy this book?

This book is packed with fun activities covering all you need to learn in your Literacy and English course.

Each chapter begins with an exciting story, text or poem to get you started. **Have fun reading**, and then answer the questions. All activities in a chapter are based on the extract and cover Reading, Literacy, Listening and Talking, and Writing.

The book begins with a **Chapter 0**. This chapter is full of questions and activities to help you revise topics from last year.

Let's try this!

These boxes include play-based activities that let you learn while you have fun; play them with your classmates, with a partner or a friend.

Revisit, review, revise

Use these questions at the end of each chapter to look back at what you have learned.

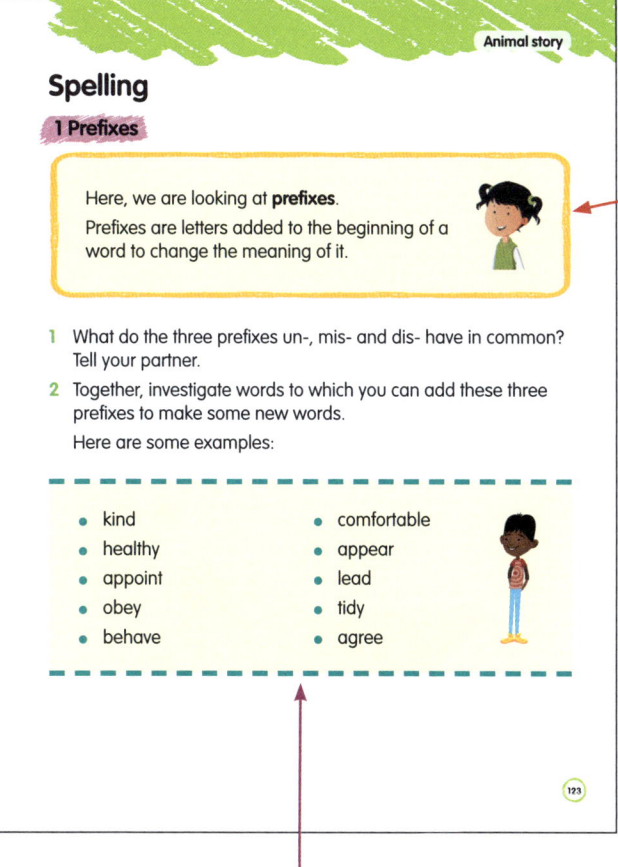

Animal story

Spelling

1 Prefixes

Here, we are looking at **prefixes**.
Prefixes are letters added to the beginning of a word to change the meaning of it.

1 What do the three prefixes un-, mis- and dis- have in common? Tell your partner.

2 Together, investigate words to which you can add these three prefixes to make some new words.
Here are some examples:

- kind
- healthy
- appoint
- obey
- behave
- comfortable
- appear
- lead
- tidy
- agree

123

The yellow overview boxes tell you what topic we are covering and give you some short explanations.

Clear examples help you to get started or find inspiration.

Remember, remember boxes give you tips and advice.

Term 3: 7 Narrative

3 Present your words in a table, like the one below.

un-	mis-	dis-

Remember, remember

Think about what happens to the meaning of the word when you add one of these prefixes to it.

2 Sorting

- Some words that end with -y have a long 'e' sound, like *baby*.
- Some words that end with -y have a long 'i' sound, like *cry*.

Read the words and sort them into a table like the one on the next page:

- shiny
- funny
- sky
- dry
- windy
- fry
- very
- bunny
- penny
- lady
- shy
- July

124

Chapter 0
Consolidation

Reading

1 Different types of stories

There are many different types of stories.

Read the following words. Sort them into the type of story where you would expect to find them.

Choose between:

1 Adventure

2 Mystery

3 Scary

4 Fairy tale

5 Sci-fi

a waterfall	a forest	a torch	a wand
some elves	an alien	a dark house	a black cat
a spaceship	a watch	an empty sign	a ghost
a map	a talking mouse	a magnifying glass	a witch

2 What can you remember?

Think about a book that you have read recently.

1 What is the name of the book?

2 Who is the author?

3 Can you remember five events that happened in the story? Draw a line like this in your jotter and then write the five events along the line in the order that they happened.

Beginning   Middle   End

Remember, remember

You are ordering five events that you think retell the story.

Grammar and punctuation

1 In your own words

Add some details to these nouns to create expanded noun phrases:

1 The _____ tree

2 The _____ chair

3 My _____ car

4 His _____ shoes

5 Her _____ kitten

6 That _____ book

2 Improve it

Editing is an important part of the writing process.

Using everything you know about sentence structure, make some additions to improve the sentences below.

1   The dog ran.

2   The children ate their lunch.

3   We were excited.

4   They walked through the park.

Spelling

1 Explore the past tense

Read the verbs below and change them to the past tense:

1   play/playing

2   walk/walking

3   eat/eating

4   run/running

5   go/going

6   think/thinking

7   swim/swimming

8   jump/jumping

2 In your own words

The apostrophe can be used for two different reasons:

1   to show possession

2   to show a contraction.

Explain how the apostrophe is used for each of these reasons and give some examples.

Listening and talking

1 In your own words

You have been asked to give the new P3 class five top tips for being in P3.

Think carefully about what advice you will share with them.

Try to use **because/if/when** to structure some of your tips.

2 Let's be persuasive

Your head teacher wants a group of pupils to create a short advert for the radio. Their instructions are:

- The advert needs to be shorter than a minute.

- It needs to advertise the school.

- You need to say the name of the school and where it is.

- You must make three positive points about the school/education it provides.

- You can include a jingle or a slogan as part of the advert.

Remember, the advert is for the radio: you will not be seen!

Writing

1 Create an invention

Task	To create an invention that your classmates would like
Purpose	To describe and persuade
Audience	Your classmates

If you could invent something for your classmates, what would it be?

- Would it help them to do their homework?
- Or maybe help them tidy their room?
- Perhaps it could help them with their hobby?

Think carefully about something that you could invent.

Draw your invention and label some of the parts.

Think about the following:

- What will your invention be called?
- What will your invention be able to do?
- Why would your classmates want this invention?
- Think of some expanded noun phrases to describe it.
- Think of some persuasive language to use.

1 Narrative
Fairy tales

Reading

This is a **fairy tale** in which Sleeping Beauty pricks her finger and a spell is cast. Will she ever wake up from her sleep?

In this chapter you will need to show your understanding of the fairy tale by answering and asking different kinds of questions.

You will learn to use different reading strategies to understand the meaning of what you are listening to or reading.

Sleeping Beauty

Read the text and answer the questions.

Once upon a time there lived a good king and his queen. They had no children for many years and were very sad.

Then, one day, the queen gave birth to a lovely baby girl and the whole kingdom was happy.

There was a grand celebration and all the fairies in the kingdom were invited. But the king forgot to invite an old fairy. She came to the celebrations but was very angry. The good fairies all wished the baby well, but the evil fairy gave her a bad wish.

'When the baby is sixteen, she will touch a spindle, and die!' The king and queen were shocked, and begged the fairy to forgive them and take her words back, but the fairy refused to do so.

The other fairies said, 'We cannot undo what the old fairy has spoken. But we certainly can make it different. Your child shall not die when she touches the spindle. But she will fall, with everyone in the palace, into a deep sleep for a hundred years. Then, a prince will come along and wake her up.'

Hearing this, the king and the queen were relieved. The king forbade everyone from spinning so that the princess would never touch a spindle.

The princess grew up to be a kind girl. When she was sixteen years old, she was walking in the palace and found a room

→

she had never seen before. She went in and saw an old lady spinning. 'What is this? May I try?' she asked.

The old lady said, 'Of course, my pretty little child!' And the princess sat down to spin. But the moment she touched the spindle, she fell to the floor in a deep slumber.

The whole palace fell asleep. For a hundred years, they all slept soundly. A hundred years passed. There came a gallant prince from a far-off land. He went deep into the forest and crossed many rivers and then came across the forgotten and enchanted palace.

He had come to the sleeping kingdom and was amazed a tall forest had grown up. It was like a maze to get to the castle gates. The guards, the servants, the cats and the cows were all fast asleep and snoring.

The prince then found the sleeping princess. She was such a beautiful girl that the prince gasped loudly and the princess's eyes fluttered open. She saw the prince and smiled. She asked him, 'Are you my prince?' Everyone woke up and the prince married the princess. They lived happily ever after.

1 What was it about?

Look back at *Sleeping Beauty* and make some notes to summarise what happens.

Each note should be no more than six words long. Your notes don't need to be written in sentences.

Try to summarise the whole story in 12 mini summaries.

Here are some examples to start you off:

- Who is Sleeping Beauty?
- A long time ago …
- Sad king and queen!

Questions

1 Look at the opening paragraph. Why were the king and queen very sad?

2 Look at the third paragraph. Why did the evil fairy give the baby a bad wish?

3 Look at the paragraph beginning, *Hearing this* … . How does the king try to prevent the princess from touching a spindle?

4 *The whole palace fell asleep.* Explain what this means.

5 According to the text, why was the prince amazed when he reached the palace?

6 Look at the last paragraph. What did the princess do after she opened her eyes?

2 How did they feel?

Here are the main characters in this story:

the king	the queen	Sleeping Beauty	good fairies
old lady	the prince	the people who live in the kingdom	evil fairy

Here are some feelings that the characters may have felt during the story:

excited	sad	proud	devastated	mischievous	angry
annoyed	loved	betrayed	guilty	embarrassed	

Choose a character from the character box and a feeling that you think they may have felt.

Explain at which point in the story the character felt like that. This means you are using the story to support your ideas.

Do this for five characters.

Here is an example:

The good fairies felt **excited when the princess was born**.

character   feeling   point in the story

3 Comparing

1 Think about other traditional tales that you know. Write down four more titles.

⭐ 2 Choose the one that you know the best. Draw a Venn diagram, like the one below, into your jotter. Using what you know about your chosen story and *Sleeping Beauty*, map their similarities and differences in the diagram. Think about character, setting, plot and the moral of the story.

Sleeping Beauty   Fairy tale of your choice

Grammar and punctuation

1 Past, present and future

Verbs show us the tense that sentences are written in.

 1 The following verbs from the story are in the past tense. Write the verbs in the present and the future.

    a lived   **b** was

    c spoken   **d** woke

2 The following verbs from the story are in the present tense. Write them in the past and the future.

    a touch

    b beg

    c take

3 The following verbs from the story are in the future tense. Write them in the past and the present.

    a will give

    b will see

    c will fall

When we are writing, we use joining words to link our ideas.

These words are called **conjunctions**.

2 Complete the sentence

Complete these sentences in your jotter. Each one has a conjunction, shown in bold.

1 The king **and** …

2 The good fairies cast a good spell **because** …

3 **When** the evil fairy cast a bad spell …

4 **If** the old lady knew what would happen …

5 Sleeping Beauty fell asleep **so** …

6 Will she wake up **or** …

Remember, remember

We can experiment with different conjunctions in our writing toolkits so that we can improve our writing.

We use **adjectives** to add more detail or description to our sentences.

They give the reader more information, so our writing is more interesting.

3 In your own words

Draw the table below in your jotter and add some noun phrases about the characters or setting and objects from *Sleeping Beauty*.

Characters	Noun phrases	Setting/Objects	Noun phrases
queen		castle	
king		spindle	
fairy		horse	
old lady		trees	
princess		river	
prince		forest	

Remember, remember

Use commas to separate your adjectives if you are using more than one.

Here is an example for you:

- the shiny, sharp needle

4 In your own words

Task	To write a descriptive paragraph
Purpose	To entertain
Audience	Somebody who has read *Sleeping Beauty*

Great writers create detailed descriptions in their readers' minds by using the best words to describe what they want the reader to see.

You are going to describe the forest that the prince is travelling through. He can see the castle in the distance so you can describe that too. Jot down some ideas about what he will see on his way through the forest.

Direct speech is also called dialogue and is what a character says. We use inverted commas or **speech marks** (' ' / " ") as punctuation for direct speech.

Mark said, 'I love ice cream!'

 ## 5 Using direct speech

Look back at the story *Sleeping Beauty* and point to all of the places where you can see direct speech.

Remember, remember

Look for the inverted commas (speech marks) ' '.

★ 6 Who said it?

Here are some examples of direct speech from the story. For each example, write down who said it and how you might say it in your own words:

1 'When the baby is sixteen, she will touch a spindle, and die!'

2 'We cannot undo what the old fairy has spoken. But we certainly can make it different.'

3 'Your child shall not die when she touches the spindle. But she will fall, with everyone in the palace, into a deep sleep for a hundred years.'

4 'What is this? May I try?'

5 'Of course, my pretty little child!'

6 'Are you my prince?'

Spelling

Some words sound the same but have different spellings and meanings.

These words are called **homophones**.

1 Matching

1   Match the homophones and explain what they mean.

a   no

b   see

c   be

d   die

e   pair

f   blue

g   right

i   dye

ii   pear

iii   sea

iv   write

v   blew

vi   know

vii   bee

2   Can you think of any more homophones? Make a list.

Prefixes can be added to the beginning of words to change their meaning.

When we add dis-, mis- or un- to a word, the new word always means the opposite or a negative.

- dis + appear = disappear
- mis + behave = misbehave
- un + kind = unkind

2 Sort it

1   Draw the table below in your jotter. Write the words into the correct column to show which prefix they go with.

appoint	tidy	spell	able	advantage	guide
belief	common	fit	obey	agree	trust
popular	honest	wise	ability	judge	loyal
understand					

Words we can add dis- to	Words we can add mis- to	Words we can add un- to

⭐ **2** Try to use some of these words in a sentence related to *Sleeping Beauty*.

Listening and talking

🚀 **1 Act it out**

While your teacher reads *Sleeping Beauty*, think about how you could act to bring the story to life.

Think about your facial expressions, whether you will stretch tall or curl up small or something else, and how you will move.

Think about acting notes for each of these points in the story:

- The king and queen are sad.
- The grand celebration
- The evil fairy casts her spell.
- The princess begins to spin.
- The prince travels through the forest.
- The princess wakes up.

Let's try this!

Imagine that you have the chance to interview the evil fairy. What would you ask her? In pairs, think of some questions and take it in turns to be the interviewer (asking the questions) and the evil fairy (answering the questions).

Here are some different ways to ask questions to start you off:

- Why
- When
- What
- How
- Did
- Can
- Will

When you are interviewing the evil fairy, think about if she will be:

- very sorry and apologetic
- very cocky and proud of her spell.

⭐ **2 Who do you blame?**

In *Sleeping Beauty* the princess pricks her finger and falls asleep for one hundred years.

But whose fault is it?

Here are the three suspects:

Her parents	The evil fairy	The old lady
They should have protected her.	She cast the spell in the first place.	She should have said 'no' when the princess asked if she could do some spinning.

Imagine that there is a court case to decide who is to blame, and you are going to be the judge.

Work with a partner to create a speech. You will have to speak to each suspect and then make your decision.

Remember, remember

Make some notes to help you to write your speech.

Writing

1 Fix it up

Proofreading is an important skill. Read the paragraph below.
Fix the mistakes and write the corrected paragraph into your jotter.

Remember, remember

Check the sentences for:

- punctuation (Is there any missing or any that shouldn't be there?)

- grammar (Are all of the sentences complete and accurate?)

- tense (Are the verbs in the right tense? Do they agree with their subject?)

- sense (Are there any missing words or extra words?)

- spelling (Are there any mistakes?).

Sleeping beauty is a storey bout a girl that is very sad. Wen she was a baby a bad fairy coming and casted a spell on her so she fell asleep her mum and dad was very sad. Lucily, a handsome prince arrived on his horse. She waked up after a long time and everyone were happy.

2 Planning and writing instructions

Task	To write a set of instructions
Purpose	To instruct a hero to save a prince or princess
Audience	A hero or a heroine

⭐ When planning your instructions, think about the following:

- Title: How to save a …
- What your hero/heroine will need
- How they will save the prince/princess
- A top tip

Remember, remember

In *Sleeping Beauty* the prince
is the hero and he saves the princess.
In other stories, a heroine might save
the prince. You can decide who you
want to write instructions for, and who
you want to save.

3 Planning and writing a diary entry

Task	To write a diary entry
Purpose	To recount an event that has already happened
Audience	Whoever owns the diary

After reading *Sleeping Beauty*, whose diary would you like to
write? You could choose a main character, a minor one, or
something more abstract (for example, the castle).

Remember, remember

Abstract or minor characters do not speak in the story. Picking them for this activity will make it trickier.

Here are some examples:

Characters	More abstract choices
Sleeping Beauty	The spindle
The old lady	One of the trees in the forest
One of the fairies	The palace
The king	One of the servants
The queen	One of the animals
The prince	

Use these points in planning your diary entry:

- What greeting will you open your diary entry with? Think about who you are writing as and how they would write.

- What will your first line be? How will you bring your diary entry to life?

- Which events will you recount?

- Will you ask your diary a question?

- How will you end your diary entry?

Remember, remember

When planning your diary entry, think about the following:

- You are writing in role as your chosen character, so you will use 'I'.

- As the event has already happened, you will write in the past tense. (Remember some verbs are regular and some are irregular.)

- This is an informal piece of writing so you can write in a chatty style (for example, You will never believe this but …).

- You need to write about the events that have happened, but this is not a story. Think carefully about how you will do this.

- Your diary entry will need a greeting (how you will start the entry) and an ending (how you will close the diary entry).

4 Writing a letter

Task	To write a letter from the king and queen
Purpose	To thank the prince for waking up their daughter
Audience	The prince

When we write a letter, we need to think about *who* we are writing to and to make sure that our language is right for the audience.

Remember, remember

Think about how you will structure your ideas for a letter. You need to write in sections or paragraphs. When planning your letter, think about the following:

- What is your address?
- What is the date of the letter?
- How will you start your letter? (What greeting will you use?)
- What is your reason for writing? (What is your first line?)
- Why are you thanking the prince?
- How will you end your letter?
- Will you include a PS?

Revisit, review, revise

Go back to pages 14–15 to help you answer these questions.

Reading

1 Can you remember five events that happened in *Sleeping Beauty* in the order that they happened? Draw a line like this in your jotter and write the events on the line.

Beginning   Middle   End

Grammar and punctuation

2 Use these conjunctions in some sentences based on *Sleeping Beauty*.

> so   and   but   because   when   or

Spelling

3 Sammy is stuck with her homework. Can you help her?

> *What is a homophone? Please can you explain and give me some examples?*

Listening and talking

4 Who do you think is to blame for what happened to the princess in *Sleeping Beauty*?
Choose one of the three suspects and give two reasons for your decision.

Writing

5 At the end of *Sleeping Beauty*, the prince and princess get married. Imagine what their wedding would be like, and write a short description of it. You could write about their clothes, the food or even the place they got married. Remember to use adjectives to add extra detail.

2 Non-fiction
Explanation texts

Reading

This text is an **explanation** which focuses mainly on the sense of touch.

FACT FILE

How do your senses work?

Your body has lots of ways of finding out about the world around you. It uses things called senses. You have five main senses. You can touch with your skin, see with your eyes, hear with your ears, taste with your tongue and smell with your nose. You use one or more of your senses to discover everything you know about the world around you.

→

Your eyes, ears, skin, nose and tongue send messages to your brain. The messages travel along pathways called nerves. Your brain gets the message and decides what to do.

How does touch work?

Your skin can feel things that it touches so you know more about what you are touching. Your body can tell whether something is hot or cold, soft or hard, tickly or scratchy, heavy or light and many other feelings and sensations.

Your skin can feel because it has lots of tiny touch receptors. These are tiny cells that respond when you touch something. They feel different things and can then send messages to your brain.

Some parts of your body are better at feeling than others because they have lots of touch receptors in them. These parts of your body, like your mouth and lips, the palms of your hands and the soles of your feet, can feel very well.

What happens inside the body when a bee stings someone?

1 The bee stings the girl's hand.

2 The touch receptors in her skin send messages along the nerves in her arm to her spine. Inside her spine is her spinal cord.

3 The messages zoom up her spinal cord to her brain.

4 Her brain tells her hand that she has been hurt.

5 Messages rush from her brain back down different nerves in her arm telling her to pull her hand away. At the same time, messages rush to her mouth so she says 'ouch'.

1 What does it mean?

1 Draw a table like the one below in your jotter. Look back at the explanation *How do your senses work?* and jot down any words that are unfamiliar to you in the first column of your table.

These may be words that you have heard and can read, but you may not know what they mean.

2 Think about what these words might mean and write this into the second column of your table.

3 Then use a dictionary to see if you are right. Write the definition into the third column of your table if you didn't get it right.

Unfamiliar language	What does it mean? My thoughts	What does it mean? Dictionary definition

Remember, remember

Remember that the words in a dictionary are arranged in alphabetical order.

Questions

Use the extract to answer the following questions:

 1 According to the text, what are the five main senses?

2 Use the text to explain what nerves are.

⭐ **3** Look at the section headed *How does touch work?*. What do touch receptors do?

⭐ **4** *Some parts of your body are better at feeling than others because they have lots of touch receptors in them.*

Read the sentence above. Which two words means the same as 'many'?

5 Look at the section headed *What happens inside the body when a bee stings someone?*. The writer uses two different words to describe how the messages move. Write down both of them.

2 True or false?

Here are some statements about *How do your senses work?*.

1 Read each statement and decide if it is true or false.

a We have four senses.

b Our brain gets the messages and decides what to do.

c Touch receptors are medium-sized cells.

d Palms of hands and soles of feet do not have many touch receptors.

e The spinal cord is inside the spine.

f Messages travel slowly to the brain.

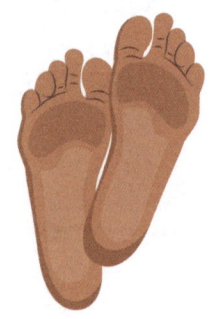

★ 2 If the statement is false, provide the evidence from the text to prove it.

★ **3 Sum it up**

So, how do your senses work?

Imagine you have to answer this question using only five sentences.

Summarise the most important information from the extract in five precise sentences.

Grammar and punctuation

Here are some of the conjunctions that we can use in an explanation:

> because   if   when

They are **subordinating** conjunctions and can be used at the start of a sentence or in the middle of a sentence:

- The body is amazing **because** there are so many parts that work together.

- **Because** there are so many parts that work together, the body is amazing.

1 Using conjunctions

🚀 1 Look back at *How do your senses work?* and identify all the conjunctions with a partner.

⭐ 2 Use **because**, **if** and **when** to write three sentences based on the extract.

Write each sentence both ways, as in the example above, to show that you know how the subordinating conjunction works.

2 Using commas in a list

This sentence from *How do your senses work?* uses commas in a list:

You can touch with your skin, see with your eyes, hear with your ears, taste with your tongue and smell with your nose.

Read the four sentences below. Choose the one that uses commas in a list correctly.

1 Your body can tell, when something is hot, cold, soft, hard, tickly or scratchy.

2 Your body can tell when something is hot, cold soft, hard tickly or scratchy.

3 Your body can tell when something is hot, cold, soft, hard, tickly, or scratchy.

4 Your body can tell when something is hot, cold, soft, hard, tickly or, scratchy.

3 Fix it up

Proofreading is an important step in the writing process. Proofread the paragraph below and write it into your jotter, fixing any mistakes that you find.

Remember, remember

You are looking for:

- punctuation (Is the correct punctuation used?)
- tense (Is the correct tense used?)
- grammar (Are all of the sentences grammatically accurate?)
- spelling (Are there any spelling mistakes?)
- sense (Do all of the sentences make sense?)

Your body has lot's of ways of finding out about the world around you. it uses things called sences. You have five main sences. These are nown as touch smell, sight, taste and hearing. you use one or more of your senses to discover everthing you know abiut the world around you. our eyes, noses and tongues send message to the Brain. The messages travel along paffways called Nerves. Your brain gets the message and decides what to doing.

We can use the conjunction **and** to join phrases or clauses.

★ ## 4 Sort it

Read the sentences below. Spot the verbs and identify if **and** is joining a phrase or a clause.

1 Our senses are touch, hearing, smell, taste and sight.

2 We have five senses and we use them every day.

3 The bee stings the girl and her touch receptors send messages to the brain.

4 The brain tells the arm to pull away and stop.

Spelling

The **apostrophe** has two jobs: possession/ownership and contraction:

Contraction: **I've** got a book.

Possession: It is **Maddy's** book!

1 Using contractions

1 Write the root words for these contractions:

a I've

b couldn't

c shan't

d you've

2 Write the contractions for these root words:

   a I am

   b do not

   c he is

   d we are

A **syllable** is a beat of sound in a word. It can sometimes be part of a word, or a whole word. Try clapping the syllables in a word.

Counting syllables helps us to spell. We can break words down into their syllables so that we can spell each part of the word correctly.

---

2 Using syllables

Read the words below. For each word, count the number of syllables and then split the word into syllables. The first one has been done for you.

1 senses has two syllables, so *sen-ses*

2 messages   6 spinal

3 pathways   7 palms

4 receptors   8 soles

5 response   9 very

Listening and talking

Let's try this!

Imagine a team from a TV channel coming to your school to interview children about their scientific knowledge.

To help them prepare for their interviews, you are interviewing some of your classmates about how our senses work.

- What would be the best questions to ask your classmates about how they think our senses work?
- Think about different ways to start a question.

1 In your own words

Imagine that you are a tiny touch receptor.

Using all of the information from *How do your senses work?*, make notes about yourself.

Remember, remember

You might want to use these headings to organise your ideas:

- What are you?
- What can you do?
- Where are you found?
- What are your strengths?
- Why do humans need you?
- What would happen if you weren't there?

When you have finished your notes, have a go at presenting your ideas to the class. Remember you are speaking as a tiny touch receptor, so you will need to speak in the first person, using 'I'.

Have fun!

2 Act it out

Using your notes from 1 *In your own words*, bring your performance to life as a tiny touch receptor. Make some notes for your performance.

Remember, remember

Here are some points to think about:

- How will you stand?
- Will you move around/do any actions?
- How will you change your facial expressions to match your mood?
- Will you change your tone or volume to match what you are saying?
- Will you use any gestures?

Writing

1 Annotating text

 With a partner, find and annotate a copy of *How do your senses work?*.

Mark the following features in the text:

- Headings
- Questions
- Paragraphs
- Introduction
- List
- Diagram

2 Planning and writing an explanation

Task	To plan an alternative explanation
Purpose	To explain how one of the senses works
Audience	Children your age (Use *How do your senses work?* as a guide.)

When planning your explanation, think about the following:

- Which sense are you going to research?

- What will you include in your introduction?

- What have you found out about your senses? (Which part of the body senses the world, example words showing some things it senses and how the body part does the sensing.)

- How can you explain in more detail? (What information will be in a list?)

- Will you use a diagram and, if so, what will it look like?

3 Planning and writing a comic strip

Task	To write a comic strip
Purpose	To explain and entertain
Audience	Children your age

Write a comic strip to explain something.

For example, you could explain:

- an activity or hobby you are really good at
- a new topic you learned about this week.

When planning your comic strip, think about the following:

- What is your title? (How _____)
- What will you include in your introduction?
- What is your detailed explanation?
- How will you end your comic strip?

4 Planning and writing a song

Task	To write a song
Purpose	To explain and entertain
Audience	P3 children

Work in pairs to write a song explaining how to do something. You can choose the topic you want to explain. Think of a familiar tune that you could use, for example, *Twinkle Twinkle* or *Incy Wincy Spider*.

Remember, remember

When planning your song, think about the following:

- What are you going to explain?
- What will your song be called?
- What will your chorus be?
- Which conjunctions will you use?
- How many verses will there be? What is your structure? (How long will it be?)
- Will you use a diagram and/or actions?

Revisit, review, revise

Go back to pages 35–34 to help you answer these questions.

Reading

1 Write these events in the order in which they happen.

   a Something touches the skin.

   b Messages reach the brain.

   c Touch receptors send messages along the nerve.

   d Messages go up the spinal cord.

Grammar and punctuation

2   Write a sentence about yourself, using commas in a list.

Spelling

3   Explain how to use an apostrophe for contraction.

Listening and talking

4   How many technical words can you remember from
How do your senses work?
With a partner, take it in turns to say or write as many
words as you can remember.

Writing

5   Diagrams and arrows can be used to help
explanations.
Think about something that you can explain and
draw a diagram with arrows to explain it. It can be
something that you are good at, for example:

- How to do a handstand
- How to score a goal
- How to draw something
- How to make something.

3 Poetry

The Teacher's Day in Bed

Reading

A teacher decides to stay in bed for the day; she sends her pets to complete her daily tasks instead. Who do you think she will send and what do you think will happen?

In this chapter you will need to show your understanding of the **poem** by answering and asking different kinds of questions.

You will learn to use different reading strategies to understand the meaning of what you are listening to or reading.

The Teacher's Day in Bed by David Orme

Our teacher's having a day in bed –
She's sent her pets to school instead!

There's ...

A parrot to read the register,
A crocodile to sharpen the pencils,
A canary to teach singing,
An adder to teach maths,
An octopus to make the ink,
An elephant to hoover the floor,
An electric eel to make the computer work,
A giraffe to look for trouble at the back,
A tiger to keep order at the front,
A reed bunting (can't you guess?
to help with reading, of course!),
A secretary bird to run the office
A piranha fish to give swimming lessons
(Glad I'm off swimming today!),
A zebra to help with crossing the road,
Oh, and a dragon to cook the sausages.

I bet that none of you ever knew
Just how many things a teacher can do!

1 Poetry review

 **1** Let's review this poem. What did you think of it?
Think of three words to describe what type of poem it is.

2 Do you know what a 'pun' is?
A **pun** is a word that has more than one meaning.
Explain the two meanings of these words:

a adder

b reed/read

2 + 2 = 4

Questions

Use the poem to answer the following questions:

1 Why did the teacher send her pets to school?

2 Why is an adder a good pet to teach maths?

3 In your jotter, match the following pets with their jobs.

Pet		Job	
a	parrot	i	give swimming lessons
b	electric eel	ii	crossing the road
c	tiger	iii	make the computer work
d	piranha fish	iv	read the register
e	zebra	v	keep order at the front

2 A good job for a pet

The poet, David Orme, has chosen pets to do certain jobs for a reason.

Choose four pets and explain why they have been chosen for that job.

Here is an example:

Name of pet	Job	Reason this pet was chosen
Crocodile	Sharpen pencils	Crocodiles have very sharp teeth like blades so they can use them to sharpen the pencils instead of using a pencil sharpener.

3 Pet sorting

Do you think the children in the poem will be happy with these pets doing their teacher's job?

Using the poem, sort the pets into two categories:

- Pets I would like to do the jobs
- Pets I would not like to do the jobs.

Explain your choices.

Grammar and punctuation

We use **an** when a word begins with a vowel (a, e, i, o and u).

1 Sort it

1 Look back at the poem to see where the poet uses 'a' and 'an'. Make two lists in your jotter:

   a Animals that use 'a'

   b Animals that use 'an'

⭐ 2 Add these creatures to your lists:

> aardvark caterpillar dolphin stingray meerkat
>
> porcupine iguana gorilla penguin alpaca lizard
>
> anaconda camel lion panther ostrich

2 In your own words

The poet did not use adjectives to describe the pets. But we can use adjectives to add extra detail or description.

Choose two of the pets. Try to think of two adjectives to describe each of them.

Remember, remember

- Don't forget to use a comma to separate your adjectives.

- Don't use adjectives that have a similar meaning, for example, small and tiny or scary and frightening.

All sentences include a **verb**.

Verbs are doing and being words. They indicate an action or a state.

3 Using verbs and nouns

Draw a Venn diagram, like the one below, into your jotter. Sort these words into nouns, verbs and words that are both.

read   cook   crocodile   teach   make   look   run   give
help   were   tiger   walk   maths   has   office   are   plug

Nouns   Verbs

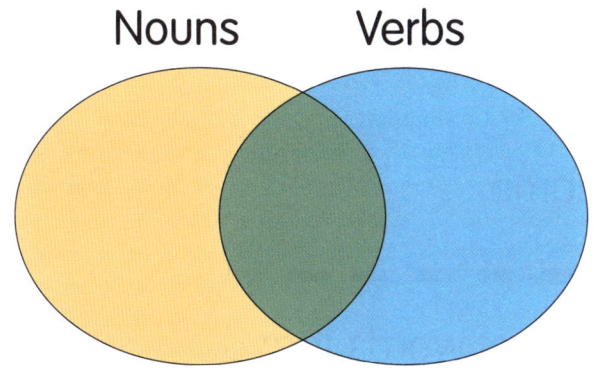

Spelling

1 Using apostrophes

The apostrophe has two jobs: possession/ownership and contractions.

This activity focuses on the use of the apostrophe to show possession.

Use the apostrophe correctly to show singular possession.

1   The camels hump
2   The elephants trunk
3   The lions mane
4   The zebras stripes
5   The penguins beak
6   The tigers roar
7   The eagles wings
8   The gorillas teeth
9   The giraffes neck
10 The leopards spots
11 The snakes scales
12 The lizards tail

2 Using the plural form

1   When we form a plural, we always add -s or -es. True or false?

Here are some examples of ways to make plurals:

- adding an -s
- adding an -es
- ending with -ies
- ending with -ves
- ending with -i
- staying the same

2   Give two examples of words that don't follow any of these rules.

Listening and talking

1 Act it out

Imagine you are performing this poem.

Choose a section to practise and perform.

Remember, remember

- You might want to split the poem between a group of you.
- Will you do actions or change your voice for different parts of the poem?
- Jot down some ideas to help you while you perform.

2 Role play 1

Imagine each of the pets introduces itself to the class.

Choose three pets. Give each pet a name and write a mini introduction in role as each pet. Think about the impact you want to have on the class.
Do you want to make them laugh, cry, feel scared?

3 Role play 2

What do you think the teacher will say when she comes back to school the next day?

Will she be happy with her pets, or will she wish she hadn't stayed in bed?

Create a short speech in role as the teacher.

Remember, remember

When you are planning your speech, think about:

- why you stayed in bed
- if you are happy that you stayed in bed or not and why
- what you will do next time you want to stay in bed for the day.

Writing

1 Planning and writing a description

Task	To write a descriptive paragraph
Purpose	To describe/entertain
Audience	No audience

Using the poem *The Teacher's Day in Bed*, write a description of what happened in the classroom.

When planning your description, think about the following:

- Which four pets will you write about?
- How will you describe each pet?
- Use all of your senses to describe what the pets did.
- Jot down some sentence starters that you might use.

⭐ 2 Planning and writing a persuasive letter

Task	To write a persuasive letter
Purpose	To persuade your teacher to stay in bed for the day and send animals to do their job
Audience	Your teacher

When planning your letter, think about the following:

- Your address
- Date for the letter
- Greeting (Think about how you will greet your teacher.)
- What will your opening sentence be? (Refer to the letter you wrote in Chapter 1, see pages 31–32.)
- Why do you want them to have a day in bed? (Try to think of two reasons – you could flatter them.)
- Which animals would you like to do your teacher's jobs and why? (Choose at least four.)
- What will your final sentence be?
- How will you close the letter?

3 Planning and writing a poem

Task	To write a poem in the style of *The Teacher's Day in Bed*, choosing someone else to stay in bed for the day
Purpose	To entertain
Audience	Children who enjoy David Orme's poems

When planning your poem, think about the following:

- What will your title be? ('_____ Day in Bed')
- How will you start your poem?
- What jobs will need to be done and which animals can do these jobs?
- How will you finish your poem?

4 Planning and writing part of a story

Task	To write a story that uses a number of animal characters
Purpose	To entertain
Audience	P3 children

When planning your story, think about the following:

- Title of your story
- Animal characters
- Setting (This needs to match your animals. You could choose a farm, jungle, zoo, rainforest, ocean, river, sky, etc.)
- Main events
- How you will use dialogue.

Revisit, review, revise

Go back to page 51 to help you answer these questions.

Reading

1 Explain why the narrator in *The Teacher's Day in Bed* is pleased not to be in the swimming lesson.

Grammar and punctuation

2 Choose 'a' or 'an' to use before each of the following:

   a amazing alligator   **b** brilliant baboon

   c cheeky chimpanzee   **d** daring deer

   e excellent eagle   **f** ferocious ferret

   g great gecko   **h** hysterical hyena

Spelling

3 Write a list of five examples of the possessive apostrophe.

Listening and talking

4 What would be your three top tips for a good poetry performance?

Writing

5 Imagine that you are one of the pets from the poem. Write a note to the teacher to say sorry for what happened on the day they stayed in bed.
Write in the first person and explain why you are sorry.
Think about what greeting to use in your letter, and how to finish it.

4 Narrative
Short stories

Reading

This is an extract taken from a longer **story**. The Stupendous Alacazamo is appearing at the Glitterball Theatre. Will Bob get there on time?

In this chapter you will need to show your understanding of the text by answering and asking different kinds of questions.

You will learn to use different reading strategies to understand the meaning of what you are listening to or reading.

The Disappearing Moon by Simon Bartram

Bob, the Man on the Moon, was tidying up the space tourists' rubbish in a hurry because he wanted to get back to Earth quickly. Bob didn't believe in aliens, so no aliens could have been watching him (could they?). He had always wanted to see The Stupendous Alacazamo's spectacular live magic show and he had tickets for the eight o'clock performance. He was so excited he could hardly fly his rocket straight.

Having landed back at the Lunar Hill launch-pad, Bob quickly popped into his changing cubicle. In a super-fast flash, he shoved on his Earth clothes and cycled home as quickly as his legs would take him. It wasn't until later that he realised he hadn't put on his vest.

At home, after a speedy wash and brush up, he wolfed down some fish-paste sandwiches and selected his favourite mesmerising swirl badge to wear. 'Perfect!' he beamed.

Bob then dug out the precious tickets that were hidden in an old biscuit tin between the sheets in the airing cupboard. He'd saved for months to buy them and had even sold his third-best tank top to raise some extra money.

'Nights out don't come cheap, Barry,' he said. 'Especially if you fancy getting a souvenir T-shirt or a choc-ice.'

It was almost time to set off. All Bob had to do was find his autograph book and set his trusty old video to record the football.

→

The streets outside were buzzing. It seemed as if the whole town was off to see the show. The Moon shone brightly overhead as Bob and Barry set off down the road. As the Glitterball Theatre came into view, butterflies began to swirl around Bob's tummy. His legs wobbled as he walked through the theatre's grand, pillared entrance and into the beautiful auditorium.

He and Barry were the first to take their seats, but soon the theatre filled up around them. Then, at eight o'clock, the lights dimmed. A huge cheer filled the auditorium before it was replaced by an electric hush. In the darkness, a thousand eyes could just make out the heavy, velvet curtains swishing open. Bob's heart was racing. Suddenly, a tremendous bang and a flash of lightning made the whole audience jump. A hundred spotlights cut through the darkness and revealed a cloud of smoke swirling around the stage. The audience 'OOOHED!' and 'AAAHED!' as the silhouette of a caped figure began to emerge through the haze.

For Bob it was a dream come true. In front of his very eyes, there he was at last … THE STUPENDOUS ALACAZAMO!!!

1 How does he feel?

Look back at *The Disappearing Moon* and jot down some of the emotions that Bob feels throughout the story.

For each emotion that he feels, write down:

- the point in the story when he feels this way
- how you know (evidence from the story).

Questions

1   According to the introduction, why is Bob so excited?

2   Look at the paragraph beginning with, 'Having landed back at the Lunar …'. Find two details that show Bob is in a rush.

3   Where had Bob hidden the tickets?

4   Why do you think he had hidden the tickets there?

5   Before he leaves his house, Bob has to do two things. What are they?

⭐ 2 Looking for evidence

Focus on the final two paragraphs of the story.

What impression do you get of the show?

- List two impressions you might have.

- Look carefully at the text to find evidence to support your ideas.

3 Descriptive language

The writer uses descriptive language so that his readers can imagine what he is telling them.

For each of these examples from the story, explain the impact his language has on you. (Two of these examples are taken from later on in the story.)

1   'he wolfed down some fish-paste sandwiches'

2   'As the Glitterball Theatre came into view, butterflies began to swirl around Bob's tummy.'

3   'A huge cheer filled the auditorium before it was replaced by an electric hush.'

4   'In the darkness, a thousand eyes could just make out the heavy, velvet curtains swishing open.'

Grammar and punctuation

Adverbs give us more information about the verb.

They let us know the time, place or manner in which something happens, or the frequency with which it happens.

1 Using adverbs

When do we use adverbs?

 1 List the adverbs in the box below under the following headings:

    a When?

    b Where?

    c How?

    d To what extent?

> wickedly   almost   enough   outside   upstairs
> first   bravely   yesterday   there   very

⭐ **2** Add another example under each heading.

2 Using proper nouns

    1 When do we use capital letters?

    2 What are proper nouns?

    3 Use *The Disappearing Moon* and ideas of your own to write a list of proper nouns.

3 Fix it up

Editing is an important part of the writing process.

Using everything you know about sentence structure, make some additions to improve these sentences.

1 Bob walked home.

2 Before he left, he looked for his autograph book.

3 The Moon shone above him.

4   At eight o'clock, the lights dimmed.

5   Suddenly a huge bang made the audience jump.

4 Using dialogue

1   Look back at the story *The Disappearing Moon* and point to all the places where you can see direct speech.

Remember, remember

Look for the speech marks (inverted commas) ' '.

2   Imagine the writer was planning to include more dialogue at the following points in the story:

- while cycling home to get ready
- just before he leaves his house
- while walking towards the Glitterball Theatre
- as the lights dimmed inside the theatre.

Write down what you think Bob would say at each of these points.

Spelling

Suffixes are letters added to the end of words. When you add a suffix to a word, it changes the meaning of it.

1 Using the suffix -ous

The Stupendous Alacazamo includes the suffix -ous.

1 Add the suffix -ous to the following letters and words to make new words.

    a poison   **b** enorm

    c courage   **d** outrage

    e obvi   **f** curi

    g jeal   **h** spontane

2 Use a dictionary to look up the definitions of any words you don't know.

⭐ 3 Write a sentence related to *The Disappearing Moon* using a word that contains the suffix -ous.

2 Using apostrophes

Do you use a possessive apostrophe in the same way for plural words as you do for singular words?

Use examples in your explanation.

Listening and talking

🚀 1 Imagine this

The Stupendous Alacazamo appears on the stage.

Describe him in detail to your partner.

Remember, remember

Think about:

- what he is wearing
- how he is standing
- if he is holding any props
- what is behind him.

Let's try this!

Imagine you have all been to watch The Stupendous Alacazamo.

In a group, share your opinions about what you have seen.

Listen to everyone in your group and write down any expressions that you like.

2 Facts and opinions

Let's sort some facts and opinions.

Work with a partner to write two facts and two opinions about The Stupendous Alacazamo.

For example:

- Fact: He appeared on the stage at the theatre.

- Opinion: He was the most magical person Bob had ever seen.

Writing

1 Fix it up

Proofreading is an important skill.

Read the paragraph below and then write it into your jotter without the mistakes.

Remember, remember

Check the sentences for:

- punctuation (Is any missing or is there any punctuation that should not be there?)

- grammar (Are all of the sentences complete and accurate?)

- tense (Are the verbs in the right tense? Do they agree with their subject?)

- sense (Are there any missing words or extra words?)

- spelling (Are there any mistakes?).

The streats outside was buzzing. It seemed as if the whole town was of to see the show. The Moon shone brightley overhead as bob and barry set of down the road. As the glitterball theatre came into view, butterflys began to swirl around bobs tummy. His legs wobbled as he walked through the theatres grand, pillared entrance and into the beautifull auditorium

🚀 2 Planning and writing a diary entry

Task	To write a diary entry
Purpose	To recount an event
Audience	Whoever owns the diary

Bob has met The Stupendous Alacazamo! Write a diary entry recounting their meeting. You can either write Bob's diary, or Alacazamo's.

When planning your diary, think about the following:

- How will you open your diary? Think about who you are writing as, and how they would write.

- What will your first line be? How will you bring your diary entry to life?

- Which events will you recount?

- Will you ask your diary a question?

- How will you end your diary entry?

⭐ 3 Planning and writing a fantasy opening

Task	To write the opening to a fantasy story
Purpose	To entertain and describe
Audience	Children your age

When planning your fantasy opening, think about how your story will be a fantasy. Think about:

- the fantasy setting
- the fantasy characters
- what dream will come true.

4 Planning and writing instructions

Task	To write instructions for 'How to be the perfect magician'
Purpose	To instruct
Audience	Magicians in training

Think about how you will structure your instructions. You need to write in clear sections with headings.

When planning your instructions, think about the following:

- What will your title be?
- What will be in your 'You will need' section?
- What will be in your numbered 'How to' section?

- Will you include a trouble-shooting section?
- Will you include a 'top tips' section?

Revisit, review, revise

Go back to pages 63–64 to help you answer these questions.

Reading

1 Re-read *The Disappearing Moon* and explain how you know that Bob had been preparing for the live magic show for a long time. Use evidence from the story to support your answer.

Grammar and punctuation

2 Write four sentences related to *The Disappearing Moon* using a different type of adverb in each sentence:

   a When

   b Where

   c How

   d To what extent

Spelling

3 Complete each of these examples using an apostrophe to show plural possession.

   a the girls   b the childrens

   c the mens   d the mices

   e the babies   f the boys

→

Listening and talking

4 What or who do you think Barry is?
Talk to your partner and give them as much information as you can.
You will need to use your imagination.

Writing

5 Imagine you are The Stupendous Alacazamo and you have just returned to your dressing room.
You send a few text messages to people of your choice, for example, friends, family, your competition.
For each message, write:

- who you are texting

- what you say. Think about your tone and use of language. (You could also use some emojis to express your feelings.)

5 Non-fiction

Non-chronological report

Reading

This is a **non-chronological report** that focuses on hedgehogs and squirrels. A non-chronological report tells you facts, but does not follow the order in which they happened.

In this chapter you will need to show your understanding of the report by answering and asking different kinds of questions.

You will learn to use different reading strategies to understand the meaning of what you are listening to or reading.

Garden Creatures

FACT FILE

Do you ever play in a garden? That garden is part of the biggest nature reserve in Britain. In the UK, we have over 16,000,000 (16 million) gardens. We like to think of our gardens as our private property but, whether we like it or not, we share them with masses of wildlife.

You may think your garden is empty of birds, frogs and hedgehogs, but every garden contains thousands of different types of insects, spiders, woodlice and slugs. You might not like them, or even notice them, but these small creatures are really important as they provide food for the bigger creatures we like to see.

Why are hedgehogs our favourite animal?

Have you ever seen a hedgehog? They have been voted as the UK's favourite animal, possibly because they always look like they are smiling.

Hedgehogs are shy creatures and they are very good at hiding so they are more common in gardens than people think.

→

Hedgehogs usually come out at night. They snuffle around our lawns and flowerbeds to hunt for their favourite foods: worms and slugs. Hedgehogs use their whiskers, together with their sense of smell, to find their food.

Hedgehogs like to live in gardens with bushes, hedges, compost bins or log piles so that they can sleep during the day and hibernate in winter.

Are squirrels pests or a pleasure?

Have you seen a squirrel scampering in your garden? The American grey squirrel is common in gardens throughout the UK. The British native red squirrel is now only seen in Scotland and in a few other parts of the UK because grey squirrels are more aggressive and have driven the red squirrels out.

Some people don't like grey squirrels because they strip the bark from trees, looking for insects hiding underneath. They also take food from bird feeders. However, they are funny, entertaining and great acrobats. Grey squirrels can live almost anywhere, as long as there are some trees they can scamper into if they sense danger.

1 Hashtag fun

Read the two sections about hedgehogs and squirrels again.

Summarise the information by writing four hashtags # about each animal.

You can't write more than six words in each hashtag.

Remember, remember

Try to play with language to have fun.

Questions

Use the report to answer the following questions:

 1 According to the text, how many gardens are there in the UK?

 2 Many small creatures are important to the garden. Find two that are named in the introduction.

3 According to the text, why were hedgehogs voted as the UK's favourite animal?

4 Why do hedgehogs like gardens with bushes or compost bins?

 5 Find evidence in the text that shows why people don't like grey squirrels and why they do like them. Write a list for each.

2 True or false?

Here are some statements about *Garden Creatures.*

1   Read each statement and decide
    if it is true or false.

   a   Every garden contains
       thousands of birds, frogs and
       spiders.

   b   Hedgehogs come out all day
       in our gardens.

   c   Hedgehogs hibernate in
       winter.

   d   The Australian grey squirrel is common in the UK.

   e   Red squirrels are more aggressive than grey squirrels.

   f   Grey squirrels are great acrobats.

⭐ 2   If the statement is false, provide the evidence from the text to
    prove it.

3 The power of sub-headings

Use the information from the text to create three alternative sub-
headings for the section about hedgehogs and three for the
section about squirrels.

Remember, remember

You can use statements, questions, commands or
exclamations for your sub-headings.

Grammar and punctuation

Pronouns are words that can replace nouns. They tell us who or what is doing the action.

1 Using pronouns

Read the paragraph below.

Rewrite this paragraph and change some of the bold words into a pronoun.

Hedgehogs have been voted the UK's favourite animals because **hedgehogs** look like **hedgehogs** are always smiling. **Hedgehogs** are shy creatures and **hedgehogs** are good at hiding. **Hedgehogs** usually come out at night and **hedgehogs** snuffle around the lawns to look for food. **Hedgehogs** eat worms and slugs. **Hedgehogs** use their whiskers to find food. **Hedgehogs** live in gardens and **hedgehogs** hibernate in winter.

2 Using paragraphs

Why do we need to use paragraphs, sections and sub-headings in non-fiction writing?

Think about how paragraphs and sections are used to organise writing.

Look at the extract *Garden creatures* on pages 77–78. Rearrange the sections and explain how the material has been organised.

3 Using dialogue

What your characters say is important, and so is **how** they say it.

Look at the words in the box and think about when you would use them.

Choose four examples and explain the impact of using each of these words.

For example: **yelped** – this sounds like the speaker could be in pain. The reader will wonder what has happened.

> said   muttered   whispered   shouted   winced   screamed
> yelped   roared   whimpered   asked   wondered

4 Using a variety of conjunctions

Find examples of the following conjunctions in *Garden creatures* and, for each conjunction, explain if it is **linking ideas** (a coordinating conjunction) or **adding more information** (a subordinating conjunction).

For example: **and** – *Hedgehogs are shy creatures and they are very good at hiding* – the conjunction is linking two ideas, so it's a coordinating conjunction.

1 but

2 or

3 as

4 because

5 so

6 if

7 as long as

Spelling

1 Alternative spellings

How many ways can we write the sound 'shun'?

🚀 **1** List the words in the box below under the correct spelling string:

    a -tion

    b -sion

    c -ssion

    d -cian

magician	television	mission	politician	station
fiction	position	discussion	beautician	musician
	permission	expression	action	

⭐ **2** Try adding some words of your own.

Verbs can be sorted into **regular** verbs (those that follow the rules) and **irregular** verbs (those that do not follow the rules).

'Bake' is a regular verb: Dad **baked** a cake.

'Eat' is an irregular verb: I **ate** it yesterday.

2 Using -ed in the past tense

1   When we write in the past tense we always add -ed to the verb. Is this true or false?

2   Present your evidence by giving examples of regular and irregular verbs.

Listening and talking

1 Interviewing a gardener

1   Imagine you are interviewing a gardener. What will you ask them? In pairs, ask each other questions and reply in role as the gardener.

2   Use the information from *Garden Creatures* to make notes for a short speech outlining the positives and negatives about garden creatures.

Remember, remember

Remember to speak and write in the first person.

Let's try this!

If a red squirrel and a grey squirrel could have a conversation, what do you think they would say to each other?

With a partner, create an imaginative conversation between the two creatures.

Think about the purpose of your conversation: for example, are the squirrels recounting an event, complaining about something, apologising, criticising each other or someone else, comforting each other, or being confrontational?

Think also about the tone: for example, are the squirrels apologetic, cocky, arrogant or friendly?

Jot down some notes on the tone and purpose for each squirrel to help you.

2 A hedgehog's voice

If a hedgehog had a chance to speak to a human, what do you think it would say?

- Would it be angry with us?
- Would it ask us for help?
- Would it thank us?

Work with a partner to create a short speech from a hedgehog to a human.

Writing

1 Planning and writing a poem

Task	To write a poem
Purpose	To entertain and report
Audience	Children your age

Choose ten words from *Garden Creatures* for your poem. Choose your words wisely.

You can change the order of your words to change the impact on your reader.

⭐ 2 Planning and writing a non-chronological report

Task	To plan and write a non-chronological report
Purpose	To report and inform about an animal of your choice
Audience	Children your age

When planning your non-chronological report, think about the following:

- Which animal are you going to research?
- What will your title be?
- What will you include in your introduction?
- What will your first sub-heading be?
- What will your second sub-heading be?
- What photographs or drawings will you include?
- What captions will you include for your photographs or drawings?

3 Planning and writing effective dialogue

Task	To write dialogue to convey character
Purpose	To entertain
Audience	Children your age

Choose a scenario between two hedgehogs or two squirrels where you could use dialogue to convey character.

Start by setting the scene with a short description. Then choose some dialogue and close the scene with a description or a reaction.

You might want to consider:

- two hedgehogs coming out after hibernation
- two hedgehogs hiding from some children
- two squirrels who have just had a fight
- two squirrels teaching each other acrobatics.

Remember, remember

You are bringing the characters to life – we need to be able to hear this from your dialogue. What are your characters saying and why are they saying it? When planning your dialogue, you could organise your writing under three headings:

- Description
- Dialogue
- Reaction

4 Planning and writing a selection of fact-file cards

Task	To write some fact-file cards
Purpose	To inform
Audience	P2 children

Choose some animals to create fact files about.

Think about what headings you will use on your cards.

Think about what information will interest your readers – remember who your audience is.

Remember, remember

When planning your fact file, think about the following:

- Name
- Picture
- Heading 1
- Heading 2
- Heading 3
- Heading 4
- Heading 5

Revisit, review, revise

Go back to pages 77–78 to help you answer these questions.

Reading

1   Using *Garden Creatures*, identify the main features of
a non-chronological report.
Explain how the writer organised their ideas.
What features did the writer use?

Grammar and punctuation

2   When we are writing direct speech, we tell the reader
how the character is speaking.
Choose an appropriate word to match the mood of
the character who is speaking: for example, if the
character is hurt, you could say, 'yelped the boy'.
What word could you use if the character is:

   a scared

   b excited

   c worried

   d shy?

Spelling

3   Read the verbs in the box and think about how to
make the past tense form of each one.
Then, sort them into regular and irregular verbs.

➔

to sing	to play	to eat	to think	to walk
to make	to swim	to jump	to watch	to work
	to talk	to drink	to run	

Listening and talking

4 Look back at the non-chronological report that you have written.
Summarise what your chosen animal can do in five words or facts and see if a partner can guess what your animal is.

Writing

5 How do you think a hedgehog prepares for hibernation? Write down their top three rules.

6 Poetry

A Dream of Elephants

Reading

This **poem** details the movement of a group of elephants. How will it make you feel as a reader?

In this chapter you will need to show your understanding of the poem by answering and asking different kinds of questions.

You will learn to use different reading strategies to understand the meaning of what you are listening to or reading.

A Dream of Elephants by Tony Mitton

I dreamed a dream of elephants.
I cannot tell you why.
But in my dream I saw the herd
go slowly walking by.

They moved beneath a blazing sun,
through rising dust and heat.
They made their solemn journey
on strong and silent feet.

And as I watched, the steady herd
walked slowly, sadly by,
until I stood, amazed, alone,
beneath a silent sky.

I watched them as they moved away.
I watched as they walked on.
They merged into the heat and dust
till all of them were gone.

I dreamed a dream of elephants.
I cannot tell you why.
But in my dream I saw the herd
go slowly walking by.

1 How is it structured?

Let's look at how the poet has organised his ideas and structured the poem.

Make some notes about the following:

 1 How the poem is organised

   a How many verses are there?

   b How many lines are in each verse?

⭐ 2 Look at the language used.

   a Are there any examples of rhyme?

   b Is there any repetition?

3 This poem is written in the first person. What impact does this have on the reader/listener?

Questions

Use the poem to answer the following questions:

1 Look at the first verse. How were the elephants walking?

2 The poet describes the weather in verse 2. Write two things he says about it.

3 Look at verse 3. Find and copy the word that shows how the elephants are feeling.

4 *They merged into the heat and dust / till all of them were gone.* What does this suggest about how the elephants moved?

→

★ 5 Watching the elephants left an impression on the poet. What was it? Use evidence from the poem to justify your answer.

2 What's the impact?

What information do we discover about the elephants in *A Dream of Elephants*?

Look at these examples from the poem and explain what impact each phrase has on you.

1 *made their solemn journey*

2 *on strong and silent feet*

3 *the steady herd / walked slowly, sadly by*

4 *They merged into the heat and dust*

3 What's the effect?

★ 1 Look at the first and last verse of the poem. What do you notice?

2 What effect does this have on you as a reader?

Grammar and punctuation

Prepositions can be used to describe **where** something is.

For example: They moved **beneath** a blazing sun.

1 Using prepositions

Here are some more examples of prepositions:

above	near	across	down	against	from	along	upon
within	by	towards	under	among	beside	between	before

Write five sentences about elephants using a different preposition in each.

2 Using subordinating conjunctions

Here is a sentence that contains a main clause and a subordinate clause.

The subordinate clause does not make sense by itself.

Because the elephants walked so slowly, the poet watched with amazement

       subordinate clause   main clause

The man watched with amazement because the elephants walked so slowly.

      main clause   subordinate clause

Look at the subordinating conjunctions in the box.

Write five sentences that contain subordinating conjunctions. Underline the subordinate clause in each sentence.

> because   if   when   until   since   unless   even though

3 Let's substitute!

Look at these lines from the poem.

Write them into your jotter, substituting the underlined word with another word that would make sense.

1　I saw the herd go slowly <u>walking</u> by.

2　They moved beneath a <u>blazing</u> sun

3　beneath a <u>silent</u> sky

4　I watched as they <u>walked</u> on.

5　They merged into the <u>heat</u> and <u>dust</u>

Spelling

1 Using the suffix -ly

1　What does an adjective become when we add the suffix -ly?

2　What happens to the spelling when -ly is added to a word ending with:

  a　-y (for example, happy)?

  b　-le (for example, gentle)?

  c　-ic (for example, basic)?

When we are looking in a dictionary, we need to know what the alphabetical order is. Let's remind ourselves:

a b c d e f g h i j k l m n o

p q r s t u v w x y z

2 Sort it

🚀 **1** Arrange these words from the poem in alphabetical order:

> elephants   dream   silent   herd   walking   moved

⭐ **2** Now do the same with these words from the poem:

> solemn   strong   silent   steady   slowly   sadly   sky

Listening and talking

1 Interview questions

In his poem *A Dream of Elephants*, Tony Mitton describes a dream in which he saw some elephants.

He gives us some information about what he saw.

If you had a chance to interview Tony Mitton, what would you ask him?

What would you like more detail or description about?

Write some questions to ask Tony Mitton.

Let's try this!

In *A Dream of Elephants*, Tony Mitton explains how the elephants move.

Explore how to move like the elephants within each verse.

When you have finished, evaluate and review your own performance.

2 An elephant's voice

After reading this poem, we do not know how the elephants feel.

Do you think they know that the poet is watching them?

What do you think they would say to the poet?

Imagine you are an elephant from the poet's dream.

What do you want to say to Tony Mitton?

Writing

You can use **noun phrases** to help you describe something. Noun phrases consist of a noun and other words that qualify it, for example:

- **The cute puppy** I adopted
- **The yummy ice lolly** Grandma bought me

Prepositional phrases make for great sentence starters. They are made of a preposition and some words that qualify it, for example:

- **According to my sister**, *Frozen* is the best Christmas movie.
- **At our aunt's house**, there is always cake.

1 Planning and writing a description

Task	To write a descriptive paragraph
Purpose	To describe and entertain
Audience	No audience

Using the poem *A Dream of Elephants*, write a description of what else the elephants did.

Remember, remember

When planning your description, think about the following:

- What else could you describe?
- Which prepositions will you use?
- Could you use some noun phrases?

Jot down some sentence starters that you might use.

2 Planning and writing a list poem

We are going to write a poem using **kennings**.

A kenning is a combination of two words, used to describe and identify someone or something.

For example, a mouse is a **cheese-eater**.

Task	To write a list poem of kennings
Purpose	To entertain
Audience	Children your age

When planning your poem, think about the following:

- Choose a theme (for example, farm, zoo, jungle, ocean, sky).
- Plan some kennings on this theme.
- What will the first line of your poem be?
- What will the closing line of your poem be?

3 Planning and writing a poem in a particular style

Task	To write a poem in the style of *A Dream of Elephants*
Purpose	To entertain
Audience	Children who enjoy Tony Mitton's poems

When planning your poem, think about the following:

- What will your title be? ('A Dream of _____')
- How will you start your poem?
- What will you observe your animals doing?
- How will you finish your poem?

Revisit, review, revise

Go back to page 93 to answer these questions.

Reading

1 Choose your favourite line from the poem and explain why you have chosen it.

Grammar and punctuation

2 Write out these sentences and complete each of them with a prepositional phrase:

   a The cheetahs raced.

   b The seals swam.

   c The chimpanzees climbed.

   d The lions lay.

   e The eagles flew.

   f The tigers rested.

Spelling

3 Arrange these words in alphabetical order:

| aardvark | armadillo | anteater | alligator | alpaca | antelope |

Listening and talking

4 Summarise the poem in three words and explain why you have chosen these words.

Writing

5 Using what you know, create an alternative title for *A Dream of Elephants*.

7 Narrative
Recount

Reading

In this **recount**, Anna is on safari. What starts off as exploring turns into a nail-biting adventure. What will happen to her?

In this chapter you will need to show your understanding of the story by answering and asking different kinds of questions.

You will learn to use different reading strategies to understand the meaning of what you are listening to or reading.

On Safari by Nick Hunter

Anna was awake before any of the others. As the sun came up, she emerged from her tent and gasped as she took in the beauty of the landscape. The grassland stretched as far as the distant mountains, like a sea of grass dotted with stunted acacia trees. It was so different from the grey streets and red-brick houses she usually saw on her journey to school. This safari really was going to be an amazing experience, mused Anna.

There was still a little warmth in the fire the guides had lit the night before to ward off unwelcome animal visitors. As darkness fell, the guides had warned everyone not to leave the camp, but surely there could be no harm in taking a closer look at the waterhole? Dawn was the time when antelope, zebras and maybe even elephants would come to drink.

Anna concealed herself in the long grass, in view of the waterhole. She zoomed her camera in on the giraffes and antelopes she had only ever seen on TV before. Zebra foals tottered on skinny legs beside their mothers. As she watched, entranced by the scene, there was a sudden commotion of splashing and pounding of hooves. When the dust cleared, the waterhole was almost deserted. However, one zebra foal had been too slow.

It now stood alone, looking anxiously around. Anna followed the zebra's gaze and saw that it was in terrible danger. Three hyenas were circling at a distance. The other animals had escaped but now the hungry hyenas had their helpless prey in their sights.

Anna reacted instantly. She leapt from her hiding place and rushed towards the watering hole, blowing the whistle she had been told to wear around her neck in case she became separated from the others. She waved her fists at the startled predators. The hyenas retreated a little but they were not easily frightened. Anna found herself by the watering hole, in the open, with only a handful of stones to defend herself. The hyenas were not just looking at the zebra now; they were watching Anna and creeping closer, baring their sharp teeth.

Suddenly, the tense silence was shattered by the roar of engines. As if from nowhere, two jeeps appeared and headed straight towards the predators. The hyenas turned and fled. They disappeared as swiftly and silently as they had arrived. Anna's dad jumped from the first jeep and rushed towards her.

'You could have been killed!' he shouted. 'What are you doing?'

Anna felt huge relief. She had rushed to the rescue, without thinking that she was putting her own life in danger. She turned to look at the little zebra. It had returned to the waterhole and was drinking thirstily. In the distance, she saw the zebra's mother trotting through the grassland to retrieve her foal. Anna smiled sheepishly. She wondered if the zebra was in as much trouble as she was.

1 How do they feel?

Look at the emojis below.

Think about which character felt like each of these emojis and provide evidence from the story that tells you this.

Questions

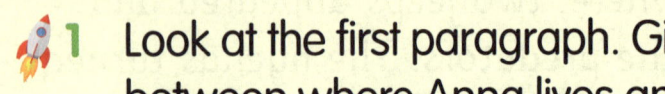 1 Look at the first paragraph. Give one difference between where Anna lives and where she is on safari.

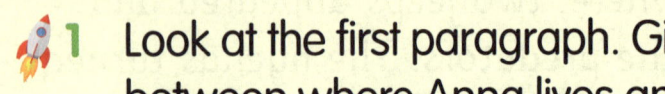 2 Look at the second paragraph. Why had the guides lit the fire?

3 Look at the third paragraph. Find some evidence that shows Anna did not want to be seen.

4 In paragraph 4, it states that *Anna reacted instantly*. What did she do first?

★ 5 Look at the paragraph beginning *Suddenly, the tense silence*. Find and copy two different pieces of evidence that show the hyenas moved quickly.

★ 6 *Anna smiled sheepishly*. What does this suggest about how Anna is feeling?

2 What is Anna like?

What impression do you get of Anna?

Look carefully at the story *On Safari* to find evidence to support your ideas.

In your jotter, draw a table like the one below to record your answers.

Impression	Evidence from the story

3 What happens next?

Look at the final sentence in the story, 'She wondered if the zebra was in as much trouble as she was.'

What do you think will happen next?

- What will happen next for Anna?

- What will happen next for the little zebra?

Grammar and punctuation

1 Using punctuation

There are four types of sentence. Look at the table to see how they are punctuated:

Sentence type	Punctuation	Example
Statement	. or !	Anna reacted instantly. Anna reacted instantly!
Command	! or .	'Stop there!' 'Stop there.'
Question	?	'What are you doing?'
Exclamation	!	What a frightening time that was! How terrifying that experience was!

Write four sentences about *On Safari*, each one using a different type of punctuation.

Fronted adverbials describe where, when or how an action happened.

They are used at the beginning of a sentence and are followed by a comma.

2 Using fronted adverbials

Look at these examples of fronted adverbials.

immediately,	over there,	happily,	occasionally,	in June,
slowly,	once,	last Tuesday,	nearby,	out of breath,
sometimes,	perhaps,	in the distance,	without a sound,	maybe,

Copy this table into your jotter, and write each adverbial in the correct column.

Time	Frequency	Place	Manner	Degree

Write five sentences about *On Safari*. Use a different fronted adverbial each time.

3 Fix it up

Editing is an important part of the writing process.

Using everything you know about sentence structure, make some additions to improve the sentences below.

1 Anna woke up.

2 The grassland stretched far.

3 Anna concealed herself in the grass.

4 There was a sudden commotion.

5 The hyenas were watching Anna.

4 Fill the blanks

Here is a section from *On Safari*, but some words have been taken out. Choose words to fill the blanks. You can choose any words that make sense.

When the _____1_____ cleared, the waterhole was _____2_____ deserted. However, one zebra foal had been too _____3____. It now stood alone, looking _____4_____ around. Anna followed the zebra's gaze and saw that _____5_____ was in _____6_____ danger. _____7_____ hyenas were circling at a distance. The other _____8_____ had escaped but now the _____9_____ hyenas had their helpless prey in their sights.

Anna reacted _____10_____. She _____11_____ from her hiding place and ___12_____ towards the watering hole, blowing the whistle she had been _____13_____ to wear around her neck in case she became separated from the others. _____14_____ waved her fists at the _____15_____ predators. The hyenas retreated a little _____16_____ they were not easily frightened.

Spelling

1 Discussing

Discuss this question in a group:

Does the spelling 'ou' sometimes make the 'u' sound, as in 'root'?

2 Sorting

Look at the suffixes -sure and -ture. Read the following sentences and listen to how the words sound.

- Anna had a scary but great adven<u>ture</u>.

- The animals were not in an enclo<u>sure</u>.

Now look at the following beginnings of words and decide if they should have the suffix -sure or -ture. Write the words in your jotter.

1 plea	5 cap	9 trea
2 fix	6 crea	10 furni
3 mea	7 clo	11 fu
4 lei	8 cul	12 enclo

Listening and talking

1 A giraffe's voice

Look back at the story and focus on paragraph 3 onwards.

Imagine you are one of the giraffes watching the commotion unfold.

Recount what happened in your own words. You can make some notes to help you.

Let's try this!

Imagine you can talk to Anna at various points in the story.

Think about what you would say to her when:

- she decides to go down to the waterhole
- she sees the zebra alone
- she blows her whistle
- her dad arrives
- she smiles at the young zebra at the end.

2 Let's debate

Should Anna's dad be angry with her or should he feel proud of his daughter?

Jot down some reasons for both sides and then present the side you think is right.

Writing

1 Planning and writing a narrative chapter

Task	To write the next chapter of *On Safari*
Purpose	To entertain
Audience	Someone who has been reading the story and wants to find out what happens next

You are going to write the next chapter of *On Safari*. You should write in the style of Nick Hunter and continue where the story left off. Before you start, let's recap what has happened so far:

- Anna has just experienced something terrifying.
- Her dad arrived just in time to save the day.

Now, you have to decide what will happen to Anna and the young zebra.

Remember, remember

When planning your next chapter, think about the following:

- What events will happen?
- Will you include dialogue? If so, will it convey character or move the action on?

2 Planning and writing a diary

Task	To write a diary entry
Purpose	To recount an event
Audience	Whoever owns the diary

Write a diary entry as one of the minor characters in *On Safari*. What do you think happened to them that day?

When planning your diary, think about the following:

- How will you open your diary? Think about who you are writing as and how they would write.

- What will your first line be? How will you bring your diary entry to life?

- Which events will you recount?

- Will you ask your diary a question?

- How will you end your diary entry?

⭐ ## 3 Planning and writing an adventure story opening

Task	To write the opening to an adventure story
Purpose	To entertain and describe
Audience	Children your age

Before starting to write, you need to decide what the adventure is going to be. But remember, you are not writing the whole story, so you do not need to resolve the story.

Remember, remember

When planning your adventure story opening, think about the following:

- the scene

- the main character

- other characters

- the problem.

4 Planning and writing instructions

Task	To write instructions for how to survive a challenge that explorers may face
Purpose	To instruct
Audience	Explorers or animal experts

Ask your teacher if you should write about a specific topic or if you can choose what to write about; for example, you could write about how to survive a stampede, a commotion or wild weather.

Remember, remember

Instructions need to be structured clearly with sections and sub-headings. When planning your instructions, think about the following:

- What is your title?
- What is in your 'You will need' section?
- What will be in your numbered 'How to' section?
- What time adverbials will you use?
- Will you include a trouble-shooting section?
- Will you include a 'top tips' section?

Revisit, review, revise

Go back to pages 106–108 to help you answer these questions.

Reading

1   In your jotter, write these events in the order that they happened in the story.

- The zebra foal was rejoined by its mother.
- Anna blew her whistle at the hyenas.
- The zebras were drinking by the waterhole.
- Anna took photos of the animals at the waterhole.

Grammar and punctuation

2   Using the context of the story *On Safari*, copy and complete each of these sentences.

They all begin with a fronted adverbial.

a   In the distance,

b   Suddenly,

c   Before she knew it,

d   Bravely,

e   As darkness fell,

Spelling

3 List five words that sound like 'u' but are spelt with 'ou'.

Listening and talking

4 Imagine you are one of the hyenas. What is your story? Talk to your partner about your ideas.

- You were circling at a distance.

- You observed a small girl blowing a whistle and waving her fists, so you moved back.

- You began to creep closer and show your sharp teeth.

Writing

5 When Anna gets back, she sends her friend some text messages.
Complete the conversation (with at least two more messages from each person):

Anna (at 10.15 am): *You will never guess what happened to me.*

Bal (at 10.22 am): *WOW! Early text! But, I think there is a time difference. U OK?*

8 Non-fiction
Persuasive texts

Reading

This text is a three-page **online advert** advertising Dragons' Kingdom. Will you be tempted to spend the day there?

In this chapter you will need to show your understanding of the text by answering and asking different kinds of questions.

You will learn to use different reading strategies to understand the meaning of what you are listening to or reading.

Dragons' Kingdom

1 Text features

1   What features can you identify from the advert for Dragons' Kingdom? Write one list for the first page and one for the second and third pages.

2   Do any of these features appear on all the pages?

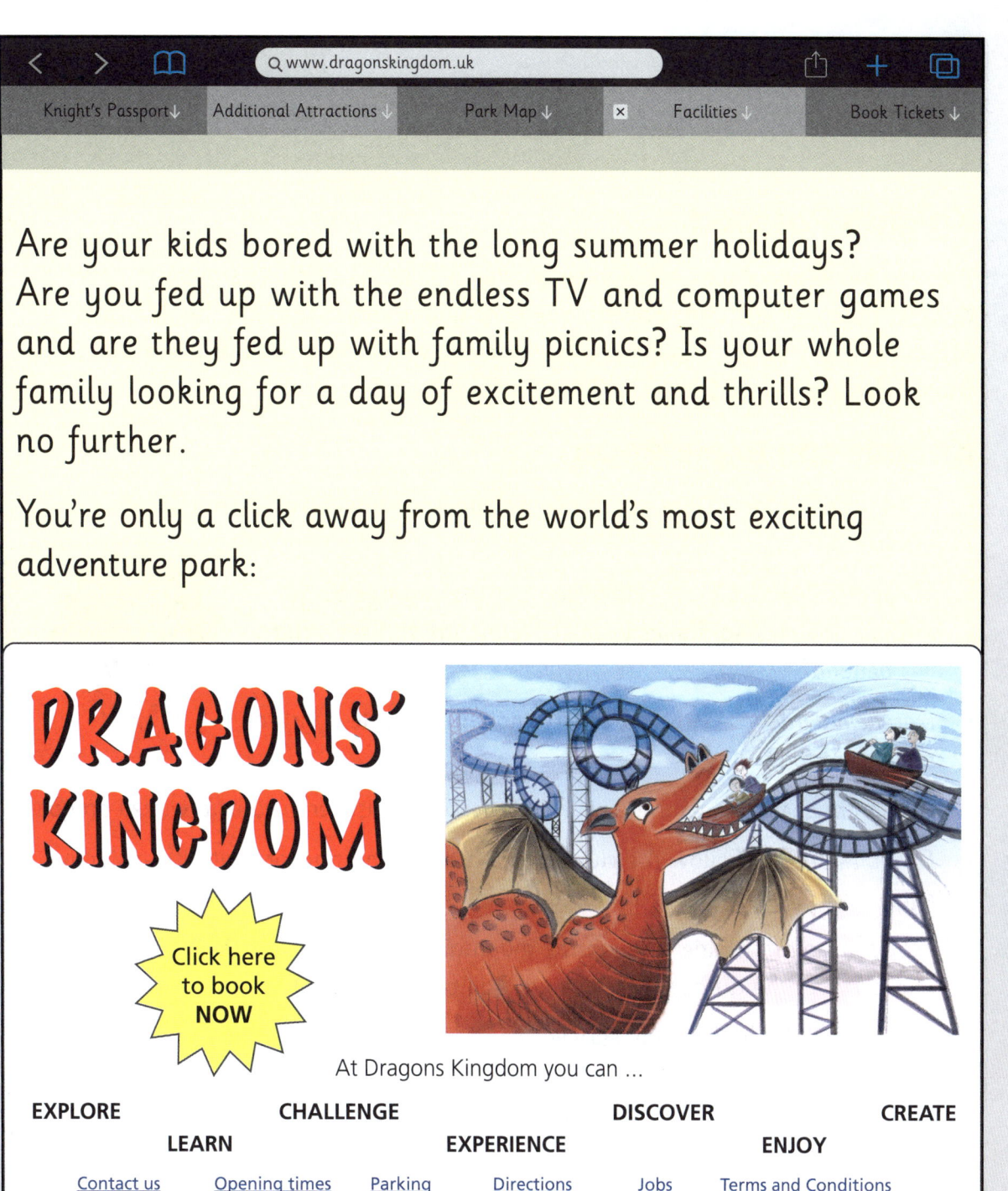

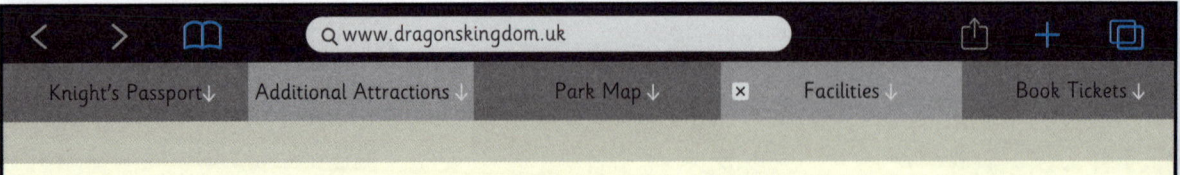

www.dragonskingdom.uk

Knight's Passport↓   Additional Attractions ↓   Park Map ↓   ✕   Facilities ↓   Book Tickets ↓

Knight's Passport

Are you brave and daring enough to become a KNIGHT? Collect stamps in your Knight's Passport and earn bravery points as you progress through the rides and activities. If you've got enough courage and show true spirit, you will receive a framed certificate and Dragon's Kingdom Knighthood!

Knights can experience:

- *Dragon's Throat* – Dare you brave a dangerous ride deep down a dragon's throat?

- *Dragon's Den Explorer* – Have you got the courage to go through the chilling flames in the cave mouth and see what lies beyond?

- *Daredevil Dragon* – Are you expert enough to battle a virtual reality dragon?

- *Castle Conqueror* – Challenge yourself to rescue a prisoner, held by a wicked dragon.

- *Dragon's Trails* – Follow the clues to the dragons' nesting site with its exploding eggs – but beware, the dragons could still be lying in wait.

- *Dragon Splash* – Ride through the mountains on a nerve-wracking rollercoaster and discover the dragon's lair behind a glittering waterfall.

Warning! Only the best will survive!

* Knights must be 1.00m tall to ride the rollercoasters and 1.3m tall to ride unaccompanied. All health problems (including heart and lung diseases or back and neck complaints) must be declared to the attendant before commencing the ride.

Click here to book NOW

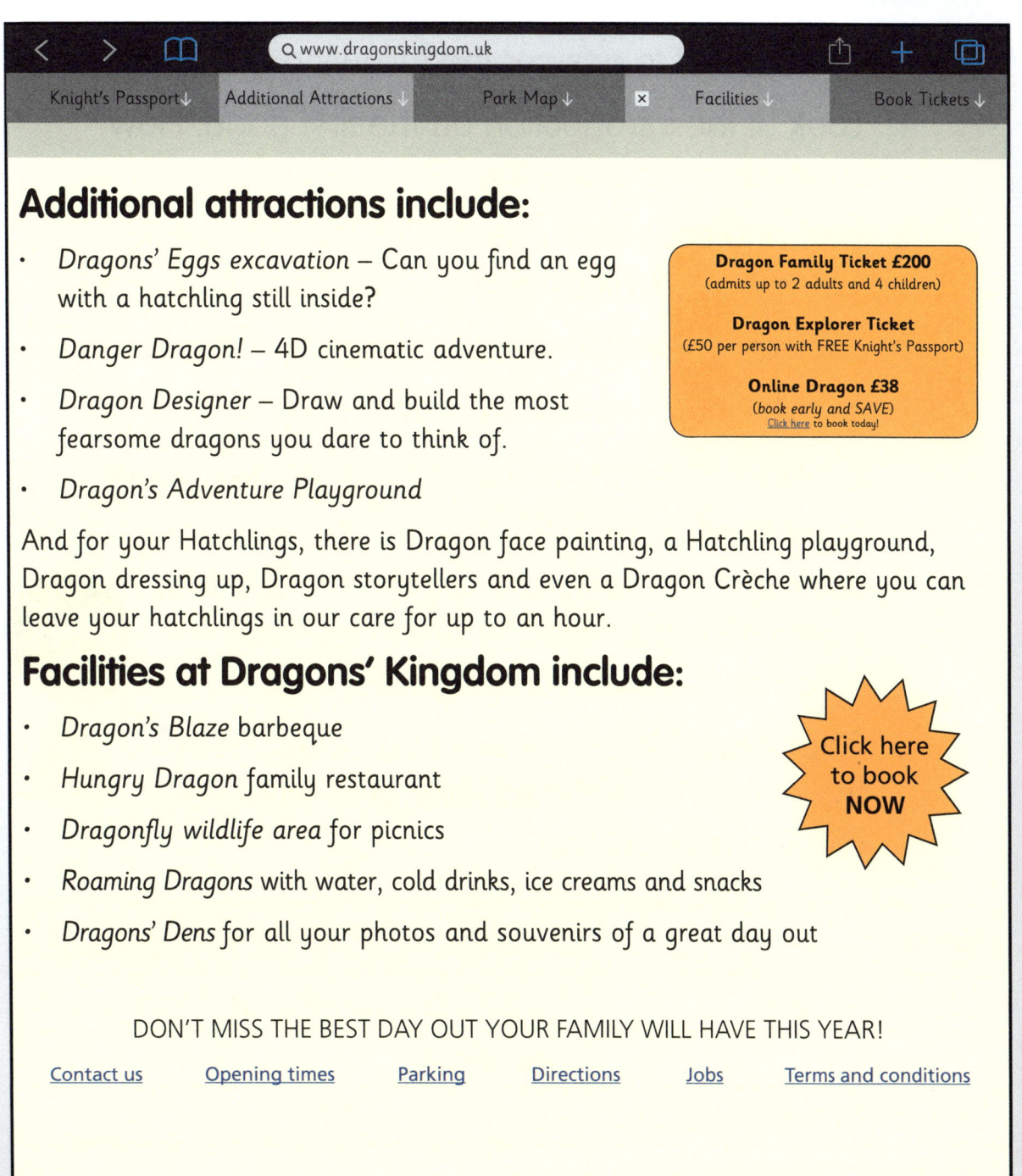

www.dragonskingdom.uk

Knight's Passport ↓   Additional Attractions ↓   Park Map ↓   ✕ Facilities ↓   Book Tickets ↓

Additional attractions include:

- *Dragons' Eggs excavation* – Can you find an egg with a hatchling still inside?

- *Danger Dragon!* – 4D cinematic adventure.

- *Dragon Designer* – Draw and build the most fearsome dragons you dare to think of.

- *Dragon's Adventure Playground*

And for your Hatchlings, there is Dragon face painting, a Hatchling playground, Dragon dressing up, Dragon storytellers and even a Dragon Crèche where you can leave your hatchlings in our care for up to an hour.

Dragon Family Ticket £200
(admits up to 2 adults and 4 children)

Dragon Explorer Ticket
(£50 per person with FREE Knight's Passport)

Online Dragon £38
(book early and SAVE)
Click here to book today!

Facilities at Dragons' Kingdom include:

- *Dragon's Blaze* barbeque

- *Hungry Dragon* family restaurant

- *Dragonfly wildlife area* for picnics

- *Roaming Dragons* with water, cold drinks, ice creams and snacks

- *Dragons' Dens* for all your photos and souvenirs of a great day out

Click here to book **NOW**

DON'T MISS THE BEST DAY OUT YOUR FAMILY WILL HAVE THIS YEAR!

Contact us   Opening times   Parking   Directions   Jobs   Terms and conditions

Questions

Use the advert to answer the following questions:

 1 Look at the introduction on the first page. How many questions are there?

 2 Find and copy two words from the introduction that show how kids might be feeling this summer.

 3 Look at the section headed *Knight's Passport*.

     a What can you collect in your Knight's Passport?

     b What can you earn as you progress through rides and activities?

4 Look at the *Knights can experience* section. How tall do you need to be to ride the rollercoaster unaccompanied?

5 Copy the table below into your jotter. Fill in the names of all the facilities and what you will find at each one.

Name	Facility
Dragon's Dens	for all your photos and souvenirs
	barbecue
Dragonfly wildlife area	
Roaming Dragons	
	family restaurant

Remember, remember

The facilities are the things you can do and places you can visit when you are at the park.

2 True or false?

Here are some statements about Dragons' Kingdom.

Read each statement and decide if it is true or false. If the statement is false, provide the evidence from the text to prove it.

1 A Dragon Family Ticket costs £200 for two adults and three children.

2 Dragon Splash is a rollercoaster.

3 If you have back problems, you do not need to tell anyone before you go on a ride.

4 There are no height restrictions for the rollercoasters.

5 There is a dragon crèche for younger children.

6 At Castle Conqueror, you can battle a virtual reality dragon.

★ ## 3 Word choice

Find the section that begins, 'And for your Hatchlings'.

Why does the writer use the word 'Hatchlings' here?

Explain your answer fully.

Grammar and punctuation

A **language scale** positions words from the same word family depending on their meaning.

1 Powerful vocabulary

All of these words or groups of words have a similar meaning.

> good   mind-blowing   outstanding   amazing
> once-in-a-lifetime   superb   enjoyable   fantastic
>   the best   excellent   magnificent

In your jotter, draw a scale like the one below and write the words in order with the most powerful one at the end.

_____

Strongest

2 Using commas

Please could you explain how a comma is used? I think there are three different ways, but I am not sure.

Explain how to use a comma. Write your answer as three instructions.

3 Using noun phrases

Can you remember what a noun phrase is?

When do we use noun phrases, and what do they do?

Re-read the advert for Dragons' Kingdom. Find some noun phrases and write them down.

Apostrophes can be used to show **contraction** when letters are missing:

I can't swim!

They are also used for **possession** or ownership:

Laura's shoes are pretty.

4 Using apostrophes

Find examples in the advert for Dragons' Kingdom of where apostrophes have been used for either contraction or possession.

Write a list of each.

Spelling

Some words are made up of two or more other words. They are called **compound words**.

1 Using compound words

Here are some examples of compound words from the advert for Dragons' Kingdom:

- rollercoaster
- waterfall
- playground

Write down eight more examples of compound words.

2 Using conjunctions

Can you spell all of these conjunctions?

because	when	but	until
consequently	although	therefore	fortunately
despite	whereas	in addition	anyway

 1 Read the words above and then see if you can identify the scrambled versions below. The first one has been done for you.

a   caebuse = because

b   tub

c   yawany

d   litun

e   teipsed

f   hougtalh

g   forethere

⭐ 2   Write four sentences using a different conjunction in each sentence.

Listening and talking

1 Listening in

Imagine you are in the queue for the rollercoaster.

You overhear a family talking about the Dragon Splash ride.
Imagine what each family member might be saying.
Be as creative as you can.

Family members:

- Young girl aged eight

- Mum or Dad

- Grandma or Grandad

2 Let's talk

Look at some of the names of the attractions at Dragons' Kingdom.
Discuss the language used with a partner.

Dragon's Throat	Dragon's Blaze
Dragon's Den Explorer	Danger Dragon
Dragons' Trails	Castle Conqueror
Dragon Splash	Dragons' Dens

Let's try this!

Look at the instruction to 'Click here to book NOW'.

Act out a role play in pairs. One of you is a customer and one of you is a worker from Dragon's Kingdom who speaks to the customer on the phone.

Think about the following before starting your role play.

For the Dragon's Kingdom worker:

- How will you answer the phone?
- What information will you need to give?

For the customer:

- What questions will you need to ask?
- What information do you need to ask for?

Jot down some ideas and have some fun with your partner.

Writing

 ## 1 Planning and writing a spoken advert

Task	To write a radio or TV advert for Dragons' Kingdom
Purpose	To persuade
Audience	Children your age and their parents

You are going to write an advert for Dragons' Kingdom.

Decide whether the advert will be for TV or radio, and what information about Dragons' Kingdom you will include.

Remember, remember

When planning your advert, think about the following:

- Is the advert for TV or radio?

- How will you make the advert memorable?

- Will you use questions? If so, what questions will you use?

- What language from the online advert for Dragons' Kingdom will you use?

- What persuasive phrases will you use?

2 Planning and writing a persuasive written advert

Task	To plan and write a persuasive advert
Purpose	To persuade and inform about a place of your choice
Audience	Children your age

When planning your advert, think about the following:

- Where are you advertising?
- What will your title be?
- What tabs will you include?
- What will your introduction include?
- What is your main attraction? (Include at least three attractions.)
- What are the additional attractions? (Include their benefits.)
- What facilities are there? (Describe them.)

Remember, remember

A tab is part of a browser window that shows what other windows are open – see the tabs on page 1 of Dragon's Kingdom (see page 123).

3 Planning and writing an email

Task	To write an email to a person of your choice
Purpose	To recount the events of a day at Dragons' Kingdom
Audience	Whoever you choose

Imagine you have just spent the day at Dragons' Kingdom. When you get home, you decide to send an email to somebody telling them about your day. What do you think you would tell them?

Using the advert for Dragons' Kingdom, imagine what you did and describe everything in detail. Try to include:

- what you did

- where you ate

- what your favourite part was.

Remember, remember

When planning your email, think about:

- how you will open and close your email, depending on who you are writing to

- whether your email will be formal or informal, depending on who you are writing to.

4 Planning and writing a letter of complaint

Task	To write a letter of complaint
Purpose	To complain and report
Audience	The owners of Dragons' Kingdom

⭐ You are going to write a letter of complaint to the owners of Dragons' Kingdom about something that went wrong during your visit.

Remember, remember

When planning your letter, think about the following:

- What greeting will you use?
- What will your first line be?
- What went wrong during your visit to Dragons' Kingdom?
- What conjunctions will you use?
- What do you want the owners of Dragons' Kingdom to do?
- What will be your concluding line?
- How will you end the letter?

Revisit, review, revise

Go back to pages 123–126 to help you answer these questions.

Reading

1 On the first page of the advert for Dragons' Kingdom, there were many words listed to explain what you could do there.
Use the second page to find an example of where you can do each of the following:

   a explore

   b challenge

   c discover

   d create

Grammar and punctuation

2 Read the four sentences below.
Which sentence uses commas in a list correctly?

   a Dragons' Kingdom was amazing exciting, thrilling, superb and the, best!

   b Dragons' Kingdom was, amazing, exciting, thrilling, superb and the best!

   c Dragons' Kingdom was amazing, exciting, thrilling, superb and the best!

→

d Dragons' Kingdom, was, amazing, exciting, thrilling, superb and the best!

Spelling

3 What is a compound word?
Give an example.

Listening and talking

4 Look at the section 'And for your Hatchlings'.
Using the text as a guide, explain in your own words what you can do there.
Try to explain as much as you can in one minute.

Writing

5 All of these words or groups of words have a similar meaning.

awful	terrible	the worst ever	
disgraceful	inadequate	grim	unacceptable
unpleasant	inferior	second-rate	dreadful

In your jotter, draw a scale like the one below and write the words in order with the most powerful one at the end.

_____
                                ↑
                          Strongest

9 Poetry 3

Daddy Fell into the Pond

Reading

On a pretty dismal and dull day ... Daddy fell into the pond! Do you think he escaped?

In this chapter you will need to show your understanding of the **poem** by answering and asking different kinds of questions.

You will learn to use different reading strategies to understand the meaning of what you are listening to or reading.

Daddy Fell into the Pond by Alfred Noyes

Everyone grumbled. The sky was grey.

We had nothing to do and nothing to say.

We were nearing the end of a dismal day.

And there seemed to be nothing beyond,

Then

Daddy fell into the pond!

And everyone's face grew merry and bright,

And Timothy danced for sheer delight.

'Give me the camera, quick, oh quick!

He's crawling out of the duckweed!'

Click!

Then the gardener suddenly slapped his knee

And doubled up, shaking silently,

And the ducks all quacked as if they were daft,

And it sounded as if the old drake laughed.

Oh, there wasn't a thing that didn't respond

When

Daddy fell into the pond!

1 What happened?

Read the poem again.

What are the five most important things that happen in this poem?

Copy this line into your jotter and then write the five things in the correct place on the line.

Least important   Most important

Remember, remember

- You are ordering the events in order of importance.
- They do not need to be in the order that they happened.

Questions

Use the poem to answer the following questions:

1 Look at the third line. What word could have been used instead of 'dismal'?

2 How does the mood of the characters change between verse 1 and verse 2?
Write your answer like this:

- In verse 1 …
- In verse 2 …

3 Look at verse 2. Name two things that Timothy does.

→

⭐ **4** Do you think the narrator is a child or an adult?

Make some notes for both and then decide. You can make your notes in a table like the one below.

Evidence that the narrator is a child	Evidence that the narrator is an adult

2 Time to predict

1 What do you think Daddy might say at the end of the poem?

2 What do you think might happen next?

⭐ **3 Close reading**

Look at the lines, 'Then / Daddy fell into the pond!' and 'When / Daddy fell into the pond!'

1 What do you notice about them?

2 What effect does this have on you as a reader?

Grammar and punctuation

1 Using dialogue

The poet, Alfred Noyes, uses some dialogue in this poem, for example:

Give me the camera, quick, oh quick! / He's crawling out of the duckweed!

Can you think of other examples of dialogue that could have been used? You can use this as a template or you can be creative.

'Give me …, quick, oh quick! He's …!'

Remember, remember

- Don't forget to use inverted commas/speech marks correctly.
- Try to create five more alternative examples of dialogue for this scene.

2 Using verbs and tenses

For each of these extracts from the poem, identify the verb and then identify the tense that the extract is written in:

1 The sky was grey.
2 Daddy fell into the pond!
3 Timothy danced for sheer delight.
4 He's crawling out of the duckweed!
5 the ducks all quacked
6 the old drake laughed

Here we are looking at **exclamation marks**.

They can be used to punctuate statements, commands and exclamations.

3 Using exclamation marks

Look at these examples of when exclamation marks can be used, and then list some of your own.

1   To punctuate commands:
    Go!

2   To punctuate statements:
    Daddy fell into the pond!

3   To punctuate exclamations:
    What a dismal day it is!

Spelling

1 Using verbs

Answer the question below, and give more examples to support your answer.

> *I noticed both of these verbs in the poem. Why does 'crawl' become 'crawling' but 'shake' become 'shaking'?*

Here we are looking at homophones again.

Can you remember what a homophone is?

There are some homophones in 'Daddy Fell into the Pond':

- be/bee
- to/too/two

2 Revising homophones

1 In pairs, write a definition of what a homophone is. (You could look back at Chapter 1.)

2 Write the homophone for each of these:

a groan   b here

c heel   d meat

e not   f weather

g fair   h main

3 Talk with a partner about what each word means.

Listening and talking

1 A dismal day!

Think about why the narrator and the family in the poem had a 'dismal' day. What happened or what didn't happen?

Try to come up with five reasons why they may have had a 'dismal' day.

Remember, remember

Be creative and imaginative!

2 Act it out

Within this poem, the poet Alfred Noyes explains how Daddy fell into the pond.

In groups of four, recreate the scene.

When you've finished your performance, evaluate and review your own performance.

Let's try this!

There are many ways to show emotions:

- verbal
- non-verbal
  - facial expressions
  - body language.

Practise the different ways you could show the feelings that are portrayed in verses 1 and 2 of the poem.

In pairs, watch each other's expression of feelings and make comments on how effective they are. With your partner, discuss any changes you could make.

You might want to make some notes in a table like the one below.

	Verse 1: grumbled, dismal	Verse 2: merry, bright, delight
verbal		
non-verbal: facial expressions non-verbal: body language		

Writing

1 Planning and writing a poem

Task	To write an imaginative poem
Purpose	To describe and entertain
Audience	Readers who have enjoyed *Daddy Fell into the Pond*

Write a poem that uses the structure and one of the lines from *Daddy Fell into the Pond*. In the first verse, set the scene and then finish the verse with the lines:

Then

Daddy fell into the pond!

Write three more verses, repeating these lines at the end of each verse.

2 Planning and writing an article

Task	To write an article about Daddy falling into the pond
Purpose	To report
Audience	People who live in the local area

You are going to write an article about what happened when Daddy fell into the pond.

Remember, remember

- Include quotes from the drake and duck. (Imagine they can talk!)

3 Planning and writing instructions

Task	To write instructions for how to rescue a daddy who fell in a pond
Purpose	To instruct and entertain
Audience	Children your age

You will need to use the features of instructional writing: for example, imperative verbs, numbered points and precise language.

These instructions will be in the form of a leaflet, so think about the presentation of your work.

You will need to use your imagination, as this is a fun and creative set of instructions.

Remember, remember

When planning your instructions think about the following:

- How will you rescue the daddy? (What will he need? Will he be covered in things? Be as imaginative as you can.)

- You will need to write a brief summary of what happened before you write your instructions.

⭐ 4 Planning and writing an explanation

Task	To write an explanation as to how Daddy fell into the pond
Purpose	To explain
Audience	P3 children

This explanation should be from the perspective of an onlooker. This can be a human, an animal or something more abstract – like a tree, the clouds or the pond itself.

Your explanation should be based on the poem, but imaginative too.

Remember, remember

When planning your explanation, you will need to use causal conjunctions, time adverbials and careful punctuation. Think about the following:

- Whose perspective are you writing from?
- Where were you when the event happened?
- What were you doing when the event happened?
- What were the first signs that it was going to happen?
- What happened? (Use conjunctions and adverbials to structure your ideas.)
- What did you think about it all?
- Final thoughts …

Revisit, review, revise

Go back to pages 137–138 to help you answer these questions.

Reading

1 Did any words rhyme in *Daddy Fell into the Pond*? Make a note of them and explain what they add to the poem.

→

Grammar and punctuation

2 Explain how the exclamation mark is used in different ways below. What is its function in each sentence?

   a I cannot believe that we won!

   b What an amazing game that was!

Spelling

3 The words 'to', 'too' and 'two' are homophones and so are 'there', 'their' and 'they're'.
Explain what they all mean and how they are used in context.

Listening and talking

4 How would you react if you saw Daddy falling into the pond?
Explain to a partner, with details.

Writing

5 Write a new, final verse to the poem.
You could use the structure of one of the other verses to help you.
Think about what you will say and how you will say it.

Information for teachers

High-quality texts have been chosen to sit at the heart of this series. The texts have been selected based on how well they interest children, and as tools to teach the Literacy and English curriculum for each year group.

Activities for **Reading**; **Grammar and punctuation**; **Spelling**; **Listening and talking** and **Writing** have been planned from these high-quality texts. Grammar and punctuation are taught in the context of the text chosen for that chapter.

All of the writing activities include **a Task/Purpose/Audience grid** to ensure coverage of writing opportunities; to support teacher subject knowledge and to provide purposeful and meaningful writing tasks.

Throughout the series, there is a range of **narrative**, **non-fiction** and **poetry** texts to **engage readers** and **inspire writers**.

Progression is built in through choice of texts and variety of activities, and questions for differentiation have been flagged throughout:

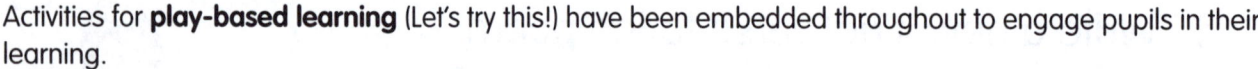

- Easier questions/activities, or building blocks, are flagged by this icon.

- Hard questions are signposted by the star icon.

Activities for **play-based learning** (Let's try this!) have been embedded throughout to engage pupils in their learning.

Finally, each book begins with a **Chapter 0**, revisiting skills from the previous year. **Revisit, review, revise** questions at the end of each chapter allow pupils to test or consolidate knowledge – the TeeJay way!

Why use this approach?

Teaching our daily English objectives through one high-quality text (per chapter) means that pupils (and their teacher) can make meaningful links between all of the teaching skills.

This approach is best described as **Reading skills developed into writing skills**. The chapters are planned so that pupils are submerged in the text first, where the reading activities embed comprehension and analytical reading skills.

The pupils really get to know the text, the vocabulary and how the writing is organised. This knowledge is then built upon as the writing skills lessons focus on teaching the grammar in a context. Giving the grammar meaning and purpose is crucial to embed the learning.

A wide range of writing activities linked to the text then allow the pupils to apply all of their skills by planning, writing and carrying out tasks to practise editing and proofreading.

Listening and talking activities allow pupils to rehearse orally before they write and, crucially, to have fun and play with the English language so that they are confident and inspired to write!

Answers for exercises can be found at **www.hoddergibson.co.uk/teejay-literacy-answers-1C**

Coverage

Chapter	Grammar and punctuation	Phonics and spelling	Writing purposes
1 Narrative: Fairy tales	• past, present and future tense • conjunctions review • noun phrases • description • direct speech	• homophones • prefixes: un-, mis- and dis-	• proofread • instruct • recount – diary • thank – letter
2 Non-fiction: Explanation texts	• because, if, when • commas in a list • proofreading • 'and' for phrases and clauses	• apostrophe for contraction • syllables	• features of non-chronological writing • explain • entertain – comic strip • explain/entertain – song
3 Poetry: *The Teacher's Day in Bed*	• vowels and consonants • a and an • adjectives • verbs and nouns	• apostrophe for possession • making plurals	• describe • persuade – letter • entertain – poem • entertain – narrative
4 Narrative: Short stories	• adverbs • proper nouns • editing • direct speech	• suffix: -ous • apostrophe for plural possession	• proofread • recount – diary • entertain and describe – story opening • instruct
5 Non-fiction: Non-chronological report	• pronouns • paragraphs • dialogue • conjunctions	• 'shun' • past tense – regular and irregular verbs	• entertain and report – poem • report and inform • entertain – dialogue • inform – fact-file cards

Information for teachers

Chapter	Grammar and punctuation	Phonics and spelling	Writing purposes
6 Poetry: *A Dream of Elephants*	• prepositions • subordinate clauses and conjunctions • substitute words	• suffix: -ly • alphabetical order	• describe and entertain • entertain – kennings • entertain – poem • inform – report
7 Narrative: Recount	• four sentence types • fronted adverbials • editing • substitution	• ou (tough/double) • -sure or -ture	• entertain – next paragraph in a narrative • recount – diary • entertain and describe – adventure story opening • instruct – survival
8 Non-fiction: Persuasive texts	• similar words – scale • commas (three ways) • noun phrases • apostrophes (contraction and possession)	• compound words • common errors – conjunctions	• persuade – TV/radio advert • persuade – written advert • recount – email • complain – letter
9 Poetry: *Daddy Fell into the Pond*	• dialogue • verbs and tenses • exclamation marks	• adding -ing to verbs • homophones	• describe and entertain – poem • report – article • instruct and entertain – leaflet • explain